THE ONLY COGNITIVE BEHAVIORAL THERAPY BOOK YOU'LL EVER NEED

LIFE-CHANGING CBT STRATEGIES TO OVERCOME DEPRESSION, ANXIETY, INSOMNIA, INTRUSIVE THOUGHTS, AND ANGER

ANDREI NEDELCU

CONTENTS

Download Your Cheat - Sheet with 7 CBT Affirmations Right Away For FREE

We've created a superb list of affirmations meant to help you along your journey.

In order to get the most out of this book SCAN the Qr code below and start taking advantage of these affirmations.

Scan the QR code to visit the page!

INTRODUCTION

Have you ever wondered what CBT (cognitive behavioral therapy) can do for you? Could CBT strategies be useful in your struggle with depression, anxiety, procrastination or anger issues?

I chose to write this book for those who may be considering or participating in cognitive behavioral therapy (CBT) as a treatment, with or without medications or participating in other forms of psychotherapy.

The first part of the book is designed for you to learn what CBT is and exactly how it works. I will also do my best to outline the purpose of doing CBT and other aspects of this form of psychotherapy.

Maybe you're struggling with a specific disorder or other problems, and you want to know if CBT can help you, or perhaps you just need some clearly explained techniques to help you solve something. CBT is one of the most frequently used tools in the psychologist's toolbox. Though it's based on simple principles, it can have wildly positive outcomes when put into practice.

I intend to use simple terms to explain how the strategies described in CBT could help you. I've created this book for those who have never heard of CBT, and my hope for you is to get familiar with these useful strategies. Feel free to come back here as often as necessary.

Noticing how hard it was for untrained people to understand different complicated terms, I decided to write in a much easier manner about CBT, and how you can apply various strategies and techniques that will help you conceptualize your problems to solve or alleviate them.

All of us, no matter how strong, have an end to our strength. That end of strength does not mean we refuse to get up and move on, but it means we do not know how we could get up, and we do not find the slightest trace of strength, so we start to sink deeper and deeper.

In the second part, you will discover what you can do to improve your mood and how CBT can help you break the habit of negative thinking. You will also find different powerful tools for managing depression, anxiety, and excessive worry or stress.

It is proven that CBT offers tools for calming the nervous system and various solutions to manage thoughts that drive excessive anger. Furthermore, this form of psychotherapy can help you learn different means to express anger constructively.

Finally, at the end of this material, you will come upon some great strategies to improve your self-esteem, sleep quality, or decision-making processes, together with preventing emotional problems.

I hope the content found here will improve your quality of life and give you advantages you never had before.

1

WHAT IS COGNITIVE BEHAVIORAL THERAPY (CBT)?

I f we look back to the end of the 20th century, we will discover that the dominant form of psychotherapy was psychoanalysis, developed largely due to the work of Sigmund Freud.[1] However, this approach involved seeing a therapist several times a week, often for years. More recently, we have seen an explosion of different approaches to psychotherapy. If we look back to 1979, *Time* magazine reported that there were approximately 200 different types of psychotherapy. In 2010, the types were said to number between 400 and 500. Hard to choose, isn't it?

However, when we compare all forms of psychotherapy, only a handful of therapies have been proven to be highly effective for people with depression, anxiety, or stress-related issues.

Of the many therapies available, cognitive behavioral therapy (CBT) is increasingly identified as the **"gold standard."** Therefore, it is considered **the best form of therapy for emotional difficulties.**[2] For instance, in the United States, The National Institute of Mental Health[3] (NIMH) and in the United Kingdom, the National Institute for Health and Clinical Excellence (NICE) have concluded that among the available psychological treatments for anxiety and depression, CBT is recommended as the most effective form of treatment.[4]

More than that, CBT has been shown to be effective for people of all ages, from early childhood to older adults, and for people of different levels of education, income, or various cultural backgrounds.[5]

Cognitive behavioral therapy (CBT) is a form of psychotherapy that focuses on how a person's thoughts and beliefs lead to negative emotions or distress. Cognitive behavioral therapy's main purpose is to help people overcome their emotional difficulties by identifying and changing certain thoughts and behaviors.

This approach's main advantage is that it is very intensive and short, about six to twenty sessions. It was designed to be quick, pragmatic, and goal-oriented and to provide people with some long-term skills to help them face certain struggles. Furthermore, the therapeutic framework considers the patient's time at *present*. In other words, the focal point of CBT is on the here and now; that is, on problems that come up in a person's day-to-day life. In this form of therapy, the problems that are happening at the moment are much more important—childhood experiences and events, while not CBT's focus, may also be reviewed. This review can help some people understand and address emotional upset or problems that emerged early in life. The goal is to learn how these experiences may affect current responses to events.

The concept '**cognitive**' involves any kind of *thoughts, images, or memories.* In other words, this form of therapy focuses on changing automatic thoughts and patterns that negatively influence emotions and behavior.

Figure 1.1.

Basically, according to CBT, the way people feel is linked to the way they think about a situation and not to the nature of the situation itself. **Aaron T. Beck**, the person who set up this approach, described the negative thinking patterns associated with depression. For example, he illustrated the impact of critical thoughts about oneself, the world, and the future.

Moreover, he outlined different ways to target and reduce negative thinking as a way to improve our health and mood. Later, he developed techniques and strategies related to anxiety and ways to treat such problems. Nowadays, CBT has expanded into one of the most widely used therapeutic approaches.[6]

WHY DO WE WANT TO CHANGE NEGATIVE THOUGHTS?

The central idea of this form of psychotherapy is that our automatic negative thoughts can contribute to emotional difficulties: depression, anger, eating disorders, obsessive-compulsive disorder, or anxiety. So, in CBT, it is crucial to learn to identify, question, and change the negative thoughts, attitudes, beliefs, and assumptions because they are related to our problematic emotional and behavioral reactions.[7] Therefore, if we manage to change bad thoughts, we will feel much better.

If these evil and unwanted thoughts have a detrimental influence on mood, our purpose is to identify, challenge and replace them with some more objective, realistic thoughts. We basically strive to get to the level where our mind is a pleasant and safe place.

The concept behind CBT is that our thoughts and feelings play a crucial role in how we behave. And how we behave also influences what we think and how we feel. We will discuss this idea a little later.

We cannot control many aspects of the world around us, but we can control how to interpret and deal with things in our environment. Jean-Paul Sartre tried to emphasize this amazing idea by saying that it doesn't matter how life treats us and what happens to us, but rather how we react and what we do with those things that happened to us.

SOME BASIC PRINCIPLES OF COGNITIVE BEHAVIORAL THERAPY

If you consider CBT a possible option for you, it is essential to understand some basic principles of this approach:[8]

1. This form of psychotherapy aims to work with patients' problems and an individual conceptualization in cognitive terms. Everyone has a different story. First, we have to identify how different kinds of thoughts contribute to certain feelings and behaviors. In this step, we are trying to understand how the problems arose and the factor that maintains them.

2. *We need to create a strong therapeutic alliance.* In order to obtain good results, it is important to build a strong relationship and develop trust. Therefore, it is normal for the therapist to often receive feedback about what is happening and provide valuable feedback.

3. *Cognitive behavioral therapy requires collaboration and active participation.* The therapist can be seen as a coach. They are present at training and offer clues, tools, and various corrections, but it is important for the patient to play their role and apply what they already know. Actually, in this perspective, therapy can be seen as teamwork. The therapist and patient decide together what to work on in sessions or how often they should meet and what needs to be done between sessions.

4. *This form of therapy is problem-focused and goal-oriented.* From the beginning of therapy, it is usually established what the problems are, and we set up specific goals, so both the therapist and patient have a shared view and understanding of what they are working toward. For example, if the problem is isolation and the patient wants to get guidance from the therapist, you can state a behavioral term goal: to create new and strong friendships or spend more time with current friends. Later, when this issue is addressed, we evaluate and respond to different thoughts that stop us and interfere with our goal, such as *"I'm too tired to go and play with my friends."*

5. The present is more important. Basically, therapy starts with an overview of here-and-now problems. However, attention shifts to the past if patients express a strong desire to do so or when patients get stuck in their bad thinking. We need to better understand childhood roots and how certain beliefs stop us from modifying some rigid ideas.

C. S. Lewis summarizes this thought clearly: *"You can't go back and change the beginning, but you can start where you are and change the ending."*

6. Finally, cognitive behavioral therapy is enlightening. In other words, we aim to teach the patient to be their own therapist, and this idea emphasizes relapse prevention. Our ultimate goal is not to go to the therapist for one's entire life. Here we learn about how thoughts influence our emotions and behavior, set specific goals, and identify and take control over negative thoughts.

HOW DO YOU KNOW IF CBT IS FOR YOU?

Every human mind functions in a different register—some prefer something more structured, others a little more creative, flexible, and less structured. For a certain type of person, CBT can work wonders. However, for others, it may not fit as well. For CBT to be effective, you must be open and willing to discuss what is in your mind; I mean different thoughts, beliefs, behaviors, and to actively participate in the change process. *If you are the type of person who always prefers to look for some kind of shortcut, CBT probably is not for you.* In other words, you have to be able to work hard, be consistent, and results will, for sure, start to show up.

Another important aspect is the way your personality is built. If you have the habit of being problem-focused and goal-oriented, organized, collaborative, and thirsty to develop different strategies and skills, CBT may suit you. If you are not willing to spend time and do exercises, it won't be easy to get good results using CBT. Also, if you have some severe or complex personality problems, you may find short-term therapy like CBT less helpful. Therefore, the number of problems you have and the length of time they've been around will tell you if CBT would suit you or not.

LET'S MAKE A SUMMARY

- First of all, CBT is considered **the best form of therapy for emotional difficulties.** There are a dozen studies that show an interesting aspect. When we have difficulties such as depression, anxiety, panic attacks, addictions, eating disorders, anger, and phobias, CBT can be effective as a short-term treatment centered on helping people with a specific problem and teaching them how to focus on present thoughts and beliefs.

- If you are a person who prefers structured work and can invest time in your mind and make notable efforts, CBT may suit you. *If you are the type of person who always prefers to look for some kind of shortcut, CBT probably is not for you.*
- To solve emotional problems means to notice how certain thoughts affect us and what we can do to overcome those "noisy thoughts." When we find out how to cope with unwanted thoughts, we will begin to be better and feel better.

IN CASE YOU MISSED IT

**We've created a superb Cheat-Sheet with 7 CBT
affirmations meant to help you along your journey.
You can Access it right away for FREE
Simply Scan This QR Code To Do Just That**

2

CBT MADE SIMPLE. WHERE DO PROBLEMS COME FROM?

"Your thoughts are the architects of your destiny."

— DAVID O. MCKAY

I f we pay attention, we'll notice people often think of their emotions as emerging directly from situations and events in their lives. So, maybe we got used to perceiving things in this way. "That suspicious person yelled at me, and I am still very angry." Quite normal, isn't it? "I have a very important exam tomorrow, and I am very anxious."

Or maybe we used to think in the following terms: "I saw my empty pockets in the morning and felt very anxious." The point I want to emphasize is quite simple. In each example, our minds highlight how the situation has caused our emotional response. Therefore, the first tendency is to think "My parents criticized my results, and I feel so ashamed."

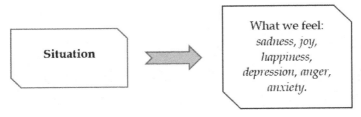

Figure 2.1.

However, according to **CBT**, our feelings in response to a situation are determined not only by the situation but also by how we perceive that situation or make meaning of it.[1] Let's make it easier. Suppose ten people receive the same news. They only have a few months to live. Do they all feel the same emotion when they hear it? Obviously not. Some of them will feel regret for the risks they didn't take; others, guilt because they have done some bad things. But others may **be sad, not depressed**: "I lived as well as I could, and my dreams came true."

Let's take a trivial example. Let's say you hear a sound in the middle of the night. If you think "There is an intruder," you are likely to feel terror or fear and respond by getting out of the room. If you think "It is my roommate, haunting the house," you will probably feel some frustration and annoyance and respond by starting a little war with your roommate. It is simple to understand. In the same situation, we can have different interpretations and different emotions.

AUTOMATIC THOUGHTS

In the previous example, the event is the same: a loud sound in the middle of the night. Still, you could have a different, quick thought to evaluate the situation. In CBT, this is called *automatic thoughts.*[2] Automatic thoughts "pop" into your mind and form the particular emotion experienced (fear, guilt, annoyance, anxiety, anger). Further, we have a resulting behavior (escape, fighting, avoidance).

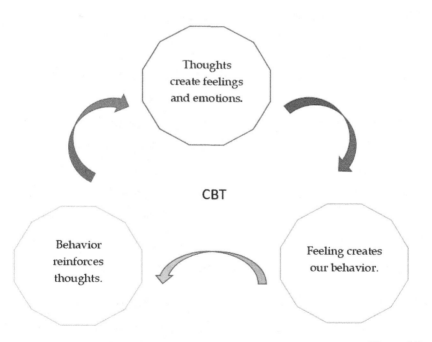

Figure 2.2.

Automatic thoughts will always show up in our minds. When someone upsets or criticizes us; when we meet the person we love; when we have great success or failure. When we wait in line, basically, every time.

Thoughts create our feelings and emotions. Our feelings create our behavior and our behavior reinforces certain thoughts.

It is important to keep in mind that **automatic thoughts** are not necessarily statements of facts. They can be certain words, images, memories, a physical sensation based on our intuition and opinion, or a sense of just knowing.

Why can automatic thoughts be dangerous?

First of all, because they are **believable.** When these types of thought appears in our minds, we tend to believe them automatically. Usually, we don't ask ourselves about their validity. We perceive them as true without questioning them. So, these kinds of thoughts are not necessarily true, valid, accurate, or helpful. Suppose someone does not respond to the greeting. We automatically tend to infer certain things about this. "This is a very impolite man." In fact, he may have had a difficult time and did not notice you because he was upset or did not have the strength to answer back.

Secondly, they are **automatic and specific to us**. Often you won't even notice them. They just appear from nowhere in your head. The problem is that we are not aware, and they appear without asking our permission. They just happen, hurt us and cause negative emotions. Because of our present or past experience, values, and culture, we add some meaning about why we had them: "Maybe I'm worthless, after all."

Finally, they are **habitual and repetitive**. Our thinking seems to appear and repeat over and over again; the more the thoughts repeat, the more believable they seem. Then, they set off an entire chain of new related thoughts and lead us to feel worse and worse.

Negative automatic thoughts and cognitive distortions

The fact of the matter is that everyone has negative automatic thoughts that pop up in the flow of consciousness. Also, most of us have cognitive distortions from time to time. Cognitive distortions are simple lies that we tell ourselves.

However, it is crucial to identify those automatic thoughts related to depression, anxiety, anger, etc. Below you will find some sorts of bad thoughts that can distort reality and bring negative emotions. You can go through them and focus on the ones that suit you.[3]

1. Mind reading

It occurs when we think we know what others think and feel about us, without having enough evidence of their thoughts. We often tend to think that they have a bad perspective of us and so we end up reacting to what we imagine they are thinking, without checking how things really are. Examples: "He certainly thinks I'm not so smart. He despises me. He doesn't like me at all. I know what he thinks about me."

2. Global labeling

This involves labels that denigrate and criticize oneself or others. The problem is that labels often make us feel bad but do not offer us viable solutions to specific problems. Moreover, we get stuck in solving difficult situations, being urged to put aside our goals and give up trusting in anyone. Such thoughts may sound like: "He is nothing. I'm a loser. I'm a failure. I am a supreme sinner. It's so stupid. I'm pathetic. I'm always careless. "

3. Polarized thinking (black and white)

This kind of distorted thinking makes us see the world only in extremes. In other words, we are either good or bad, we have done something perfectly or we have failed. There is no middle ground or nuance in this thinking trap. It's like looking in the crayon box and seeing either white or black. If we have some partial successes, we consider them failures. The problem is that we remain in a constant state of tension that often leads to great disappointments and real crusades against us and the world. This misconception often sounds like, "If I don't always win, I mean, I'm a loser. If it's not perfect, I did it in vain. If I'm not very happy, I'm a lost man."

4. Catastrophizing

Do you meet people who always expect things to go wrong? This habit of thinking makes us exaggerate and distort unpleasant situations, turning them into terrible, horrible, and catastrophic situations. No matter what happens, the scenarios are awful: "If my husband leaves me, my life is over. If it doesn't work out, it will be an unimaginable disaster. I'm going to lose everything, and it's going to be awful. I feel terrible."

5. Overgeneralization

This is a common trap and occurs when we derive a generally valid conclusion based on a single unpleasant incident. Such generalizations involve the use of keywords: never, always, nobody, everyone. When this distortion of reality arises, we can say something like this: "I never do anything right. I always forget everything. It only happens to me. Nobody helps me with anything."

6. Personalization

Surely you know someone who takes upon themself the whole guilt of humanity. Even if we have a small part of the fault, we often fail to see all the factors involved. If we fall into this trap, we can think, "It's my fault I'm depressed, and I deserve my fate. My relationships don't work because I've never been a good partner. It's my fault. I didn't know how to take care of my health."

7. Filtering

This distortion occurs when we absorb only the negative aspects of experiences and completely ignore the neutral or positive ones. In doing so, our image of life is colored only in black. For example, if we receive constructive feedback, we only retain criticism. From a series of events, we remember only the negative ones. When someone doesn't want to help us, we forget whenever they did help us.

8. Incorrect comparisons

This is one of the most common distortions. Based on certain unrealistic standards, we make all kinds of comparisons with other people, looking to see who is smarter, better, and more attractive than us. By comparison, we end up feeling inadequate. Here are a few examples of thoughts like this: "He is so smart. I will not achieve anything great. My girlfriend is much better adjusted than me and she is always praised by others, but I'm always such a loser."

9. Emotional reasoning

At one point, I talked to someone, and she was still trying to convince herself that something bad was going to happen. In fact, nothing bad happened later when I examined the evidence. The problem was that she always allowed her emotions to guide her in interpreting reality. The only argument she had was: "That's how I feel. If I feel that something bad will happen, it means that something bad will really happen. If I feel guilty, it means I'm really guilty. If I feel incapable, I am incapable."

10. Should statements

This trap of thinking involves a series of rules about how we should feel or think or behave. "How exactly should others be." Through this attitude, we put a lot of pressure on ourselves and impose some unrealistic, exaggerated standards. For example: "I always have to do everything perfectly. All people must be righteous. Life must be extraordinary. I must be healthy."

Where do automatic negative thoughts come from?

The CBT approach teaches us that unhelpful thinking is influenced by a "deeper" level of thinking, making people vulnerable to having distorted thinking patterns. These deeper levels are known as **rules, assumptions, and core**

beliefs. If we want to overcome different issues, we have to understand and fight back against this kind of distortion.

Figure 2.3.

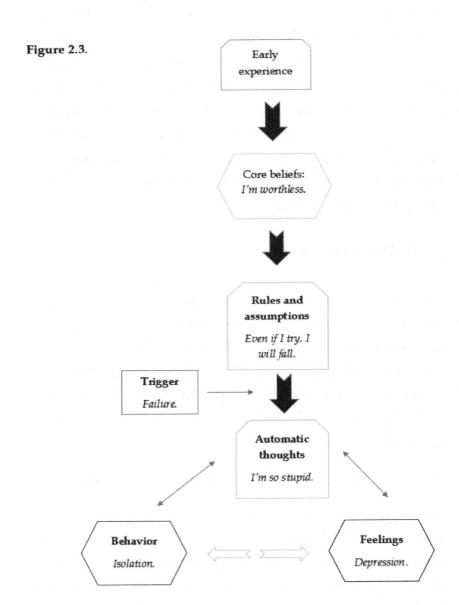

Rules and assumptions

From early childhood, we learn certain rules and assumptions through our interactions with family members and the world around us.[4] For example, you can learn something like this: "If you can't do something perfectly, then it's not even worth trying at all. I must try harder to be smarter." However, it is essential to emphasize one important aspect. These assumptions and rules may not be evident to you and may remain out of your awareness.

With that being said, having some clear rules, in itself, is not a bad thing. But we have to make some distinction between healthy rules and unhelpful ones. Helpful rules are realistic, adaptable, and flexible. An example of a healthy rule is that we should stop at red lights. Unhelpful rules are those that are inflexible, rigid, and unreasonable. For instance, holding the belief, "I must never make mistakes, no one should make mistakes." Such rules and assumptions are unreasonable because it is unlikely that we could maintain this standard, which means we are likely to feel bad when we make a mistake. CBT can help you become more aware of your own rules and assumptions and how these contribute to a pattern of negative automatic thoughts.

Core beliefs

These beliefs are at the deepest level of mind, even deeper than your rules and assumptions. We usually develop them early in life. Also, it is very difficult to change these central beliefs. When we become aware of them, they are often painful, and we tend to avoid confronting them.

A possible explanation for the difficulty in letting go of these unhelpful thoughts is there may be a strong core belief at the root of that automatic thought. For instance, at the deepest level of our minds, we may think like this: "I'm unlovable, I'm helpless, I'm inadequate." If we think like this about ourselves, it is possible to maintain this tendency to focus on information that supports the belief and ignore evidence that contradicts it.

In the following chapters, we will learn how to identify, evaluate, and change habitual thinking patterns at each of these cognition levels. Once you have learned these skills and techniques in therapy, you will become your own therapist. You will have the necessary resources to manage difficult experiences and emotional upset on your own.

3

COGNITIVE BEHAVIORAL STRATEGY TO OVERCOME DEPRESSION

❝ *"Before you can see the light, you have to deal with the darkness."*

D epression involves a significant mood disorder, and its manifestation is different from person to person. It is important to note that not all people who struggle with depression experience the same range of symptoms or the same intensity.[1] Our minds are sculpted differently. Therefore, they work differently.

Simultaneously, the intensity and severity of depression may vary on a continuum (see Figure 3.1). At one end there may be mild or moderate symptoms; such difficulties include increased sadness, irritability, loss of appetite and energy, and sleep problems. At the other end of the continuum, there may be more severe symptoms such as difficulty in concentrating, prolonged fatigue, isolation from those around us, feelings of despair, feelings of hopelessness or helplessness, suicidal behavior and thoughts.[2]

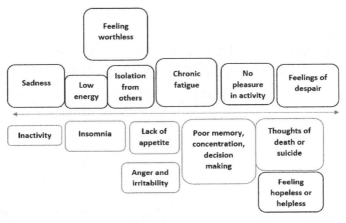

Figure 3.1.

I FEEL SAD. DO I HAVE DEPRESSION?

An important distinction deserves to be made between states close to depression, such as **sadness**.

Sadness is a negative, natural, but functional emotion. Usually, sadness occurs when we experience difficult events, especially those we consider loss (loss of a good opportunity, a meaningful relationship, or a certain status).

The main differences between sadness and depression are the following:

- Sadness is usually moderate and short-term, while depression is persistent and long-lasting.
- Sadness does not necessarily affect our own value or image of ourselves, while depression brings with it strong feelings of guilt, worthlessness, uselessness, and emptiness.
- When we are sad, we can still feel certain positive emotions, and we can appreciate many good things; depression, on the other hand, involves a diminished ability to feel joy or pleasure.
- In sadness, we are not flirting with suicidal thoughts, but when we are depressed, suicidal thoughts can occur.
- Sadness is an uncomfortable emotion, but one that allows us to learn. The mind is more prone when it is sad to analyze things and develop important lessons from our experiences. Depression, instead, can be a dreaded enemy.
- Basically, sadness is when you stumble and fall, but get up. Depression is when you stumble and fall but stay right on the floor.

Depression is manifested by specific symptoms and lasts for at least two weeks, and the symptoms are present almost daily. You don't need to experience all the symptoms listed above in order for you to have depression; it is enough for only some of them to appear. In fact, the whole rainbow of symptoms rarely appears.[3]

Simply put, depression affects several aspects that I will briefly detail: *emotional, behavioral, cognitive, and physiological* (at the level of the body). Depression affects the way we think, behave, feel, and our relationships with others, to the extent that it causes distress.[4]

At the emotional level, when a person is depressed, negative emotions appear, such as a heightened state of sadness, loss of pleasure, no interest in almost anything (things that used to fascinate us and bring fulfillment no longer represent any molecule of joy), irritability (we can break out and get angry about anything). Another important symptom is feeling excessively guilty. People with depression may have ongoing feelings of guilt and feel bad about themselves and things they have said or done, even specific events that have long since passed.

The behavioral facet targets the main possible behaviors: agitation or motor slowness (sluggishness, slowness), isolation from others, giving up or avoiding pleasant activities, and certain suicidal attempts.

Regarding the cognitive part, a person struggling with depression may experience difficulty in concentrating (can no longer read as before, is not present), thoughts that devalue their own person: "I see no choice, I am good for nothing," or pessimism: "My future will be a disaster." Also, the decision-making process can be affected. Even small and simple decisions can be affected.

At the physiological level, the following symptoms may occur: chronic fatigue, changes in appetite, insomnia or hypersomnia, somatic pain, and tension.

Can the brain really be affected by depression?

Short and very rudimentary answer is yes. Studies that have used cerebral neuroimaging and scanned brain images have shown some problems with the way certain systems are involved in regulating our mood or how we feel emotions and process rewards. There are also changes in the mind's processes, such as motivation, memory, attention, and regulation of stress response.[5]

Differences between people with depression and those without were also identified in the structure of certain regions (volume of gray and white matter) and in their functionality (glucose consumption or the activity of certain neurotransmitters). More details in this area can be accessed from the references section. Therefore, undisputed evidence shows that life's harshness and density can affect the brain in an extremely unpleasant way.[6]

Can depression wear a mask?

The simple answer is yes. At one point, I was talking to someone who explained to me with great passion and ardor that in the countryside, depression does not dare to appear. There are no such symptoms here, he told me. Later, researching the problem, I realized he was right; there were no symptoms there because the symptoms were already disguised.

Depression "takes shape," depending on how it is allowed to express itself in that specific area. Depression in the countryside is expressed differently from in the town. If we explore the problem further, we will find that every culture or region has an "accepted way" in which depression can be expressed.

For example, in India, mental problems are seen as a defect that cannot be talked about to doctors or relatives. This is why patients who experience depression when they go to the doctor report certain pains in their bodies, because those are accepted and tolerated.

In Zimbabwe, depression is called "kufungisisa," which means "overthinking."

In Korea, there is "accumulated fire syndrome," the main symptoms being abdominal pain, sighing, impulsive walking, emotional discharge, moaning, etc.[7]

Let me simplify things for you. Because we exile depressive states in the corner of the ring, they may express themselves a little differently, depending on how we perceive that it is okay for it to happen. This is called *somatization*.

When the pain in the mind reaches its maximum, the body takes over that pain and converts it into symptoms that we know better: chest pain, palpitations, pain in the heart area, and frequent headache. Do you remember that stomachache that came on suddenly when you were very upset? Or those sweats that seemingly have nothing to do with it? What about palpitations? Not to mention "fatigue for no reason."

Studies have revealed that chronic pain, which apparently has no objective reason, may be closely related to our mood.[8]

Attention, I don't want to confuse things; we're talking about somatization when the physical causes of other potential diseases have been eliminated.

Somatization or masking depression occurs because we constantly try to stifle pain or deny it, running away from emotional problems. And when the glass fills up, we all know what's going on. After all, how long can you swim through the turbulent waters?

I know what depression is because I've been through depression.

In clinical practice, I mostly attract a majority of patients who are diagnosed with major depressive disorder. I think I'm destined to be a magnet for depression. When such a case arose, I deserved it. I always listened reverently to the story of depression from patients, but I understood it when it was my turn to live it.

You understand depression a lot better when you experience it yourself. However, I do not necessarily encourage you to live it. It is extremely difficult to understand a person who reports some common symptoms if you have never felt them. Some time ago, I experienced a situation that completely destabilized my perspective of the world and life. Immediately after the shock of those problems, there were some known symptoms that I never expected. I started to feel very sad all day long. I didn't have a gram of energy for anything, and I saw every day as a punishment, not as an opportunity.

If I could sleep, I couldn't tell if I was dreaming, sleeping, or awake. My mind was running all sorts of unfortunate scenarios. Before, I used to do sports, I really liked movement, read and studied quite a lot, played the guitar, and had many other hobbies. By the time these symptoms appeared, all the pleasant activities I used to do before, completely vanished.

My ability to concentrate was so stunted. When I tried to read something, my mind was no longer there. I couldn't really assimilate what I was reading, no matter how wonderful the reading was. Future plans? The only reasonable plan was to have no plan.

I couldn't find any joy in singing, and the food had begun to taste like sadness and depression. Every experience I lived—whether I saw, heard, imagined, thought, or remembered—

the black clouds of depression contaminated everything. All the strange and deep doubts were piling up inside me.

Now those moments seem so far away and erased. I took it very hard, and I felt it even harder. *The braver we are, the harder we will feel the collapse in its time. And the lesson is simple: collapse has its time, no matter who you are and how strong you think you are.*

THE CAUSES OF DEPRESSION

One of the most common questions, when we are in pain, is: *Why? Why me?* I have heard dozens of such questions from patients, shot down by the arrows of depression. It's like a disk that, once turned on, doesn't stop. Even when we have an in-depth knowledge of things, this seed sprouts in our minds: Why do these things happen to me? Why can't this be easy?

The answer to this question is a complex and nuanced one, but it is extremely important to process the causes of the problems because, depending on this perspective, we will act in one way or another. Therefore, we will make a brief incursion into what the literature tells us about the causes of these problems.

The vast majority of diseases do not have a single cause but rather a combination of causes. Formulated in simpler terms, a glass of water is a compound of many drops of water. Therefore, depression involves a combination of factors that interact with each other.[9]

1. Biological factors

Studies have shown that people who develop depression come with a genetic background that makes them vulnerable to it. Each of us has the 5HTTLPR (serotonin transporter gene), which has a short or long form. People who have inherited the short form from their parents are more vulnerable to depression. In other words, they have a higher sensitivity to negative events, compared to those who inherited the long form of this gene, representing attention, sensitivity, and no depression.[10]

This gene is related to the mood we have. If serotonin levels are high, the mood tends to be good, but we begin to feel depressed if it drops significantly.

If we look at those around us, we will find that naturally and mysteriously, some of us are more inclined to be sad no matter what happens, others are happy and laugh at any silly thing or because today is Monday.

The main idea worth remembering here is that some of us are built and created to be more sensitive than others, in terms of how we project painful events. It does not mean we will necessarily develop depression, but we will be more vulnerable.

Cognitive theory of depression

This was introduced by the psychiatrist A. Beck (1967, 1983, 2008) and is considered one of the best-supported theories with scientific evidence.[11] The key factor in this theory is the importance of our thoughts and beliefs. The human mind begins to encode different beliefs and perspectives early in life. In other words, depression is mainly caused by the attitudes and beliefs we have formed throughout our lives, which are activated by the events we are currently facing (see figure 3.2).

From an early age, we go through various more or less unpleasant contexts that favor the formation of beliefs: stable, strong, and inflexible.[12] In most situations, the mind has not really processed the importance and effect those events have on us. For example, if I was humiliated at school and had repeated failures there, my mind can learn, "I'm not that important anyway, I'm not good enough, I'm a total failure or the only one to blame for all the disasters in my life." These beliefs are strongly fixed in mind and will come to the surface in today's difficult times. For example, suppose I was humiliated or failed an important exam.

These beliefs have never really been addressed or confronted. Later, depression creeps into our lives because of them, so you start to think that you are not good enough, and you find evidence of it. Later "black dogs of depression" start to appear.[13]

If these beliefs are not activated at the moment, we live by camouflaging them without them bothering us much. But when they are hooked by certain troubles, they can lead to distortions of reality and later to depression. The moment these cognitive schemes are active, the mind begins the battle of distorting reality. What this theory proves is that the situation itself does not lead to depression.

It is not the fact that we are going through the trouble that pushes us into the arms of depression, but the way our minds think about these situations. The way we project trouble into our minds makes us feel depressed, sad, worried, and so on.

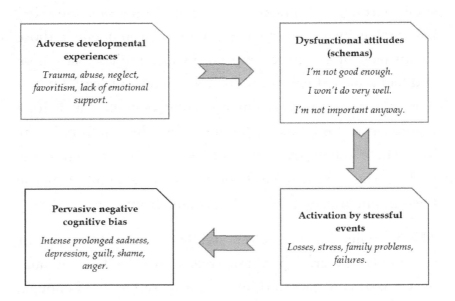

Figure 3.2.

When there is no connection between what you do and what happens to you

When we strive to do our job well, we automatically set certain expectations in our minds. When we are kind to others, we expect that people will treat us with kindness as well. When we offer respect, we assume that we will receive it back from others. If we are faithful, we expect others to be faithful. If we are honest, we think that others will be the same. If we love, we expect others to love us. But this is not always the case. In fact, this doesn't happen that often.

You look around and notice all kinds of wicked, unjust, unfaithful people. And they are respected, they are doing great, and they are making good progress. *Those who have done good receive evil, and those who have done evil receive good*. And then you start to see no connection between what you do and what you receive.

You can't make the connections any more. Automatically, what we do starts to lose value. Everything I did, I did in vain. And so, depression begins to creep into our minds. Any of us can get to the point where we no longer understand the meaning of things.

Martin Seligman studied this phenomenon called *learned helplessness*.[14] You learn that whatever you do does not bring you results, and then what is the point of doing things, anyway?

In one of his studies, he put some dogs in a cage that had two gates. If they walked through one of the gates, they received an electric shock; through the other, they received food, simply put, *a punishment and a reward*. Being smart animals, they learned not to go where they received the electric shock, but where they received food.

At some point, the experimenter changed the conditions. When they went where they used to receive shocks, sometimes they received food, sometimes electric shocks. When they went where they first received food, sometimes they received electric shocks, sometimes food. In a random way. What happened?

The animals became more and more apathetic and gradually began to retreat and no longer want to walk through either of the two gates. Even though there were no restrictions, the dogs gave up any possible option, some of them preferring death.

When you press the right button but receive a lot of punishment, the mind loses, it's confused and gradually reaches the end of its powers. Any healthy mind works this way.

HOW TO OVERCOME DEPRESSION

1. *One of the most efficient strategies to beat depression is behavioral activation.*

C. S. Lewis described involuntary behavioral activation as follows: "Enough had been thought, said, felt, and imagined. It was about time that something should be done."

On a cold and early morning, I took the elevator that led to the Psychiatry Department. I had enough energy and could not wait to see what patients were there on that day. I had shown my intention to take a case of severe depression. I was told that I had to go to Mrs. M and do behavioral activation with her.

All said and done, I thought, it doesn't seem to be beyond me. I knew the theory well. But as I would find out later, I was terribly mistaken. I picked up a list of fun activities, walked into the room, and headed for the patient. Mrs. M was lying in bed, with her eyes fixed on the ceiling. She had that kind of look that suggests to you right from the start to finish therapies quickly and mind your own business.

I introduced myself briefly and concisely, I told her what my intentions were, and the result was no answer. I encouraged her to tell me a few things about herself and what the current issues were. The answers, if they can be considered answers, were vague, monosyllabic, and lifeless. When I asked her what she liked to do before, the final answer was something like, "I don't remember anything."

I asked her about family, children, grandchildren, flowers, friends—absolutely everything I could think of in that situation. When I asked her what she was thinking about, the unwanted, short, and sharp answer came immediately: nothing.

Now her mind wiped out all the pleasant things in her life; there was nothing that convinced her to do anything. She couldn't talk to me, and after 10 minutes, I realized she was very tired and wanted me to leave. I negotiated the "conditions of my departure," a three-meter walk, and slowly left the salon. I considered it a defeat. I left the room with all the tires deflated, including the spare one. I later found out that this is the case for almost all patients who have severe depression. No reaction. But we don't need to get there. There is another option.

Why are things getting worse?

When we feel depressed, we tend to avoid activities that tire us. We believe that they will make us even more tired and that we will register new failures. So, there are two big threats: *inactivity* and *avoidance*. The problem is we avoid not only strenuous activities but also pleasant, recreational ones that we used to do because we feel that we don't like them anymore, and there is no point in doing them.

We avoid getting involved in activities that would bring us results. We avoid doing behaviors that would result in positive states and avoid doing things that have meaning to us. Basically, we avoid everything we can avoid: people, negative emotions, thoughts, plans, or making decisions. Massive avoidance, I call it.

The consequences are dramatic. For example, if I isolate myself from everyone and I don't meet anyone because I feel depressed, the consequence is that I will feel more and more lonely, and I will deduce that no one cares about me. Moreover, I will avoid others until they start avoiding me. And this is exactly how we stepped into the vicious circles of avoidance.

The bottom line is that what we feel often comes from what we do. If you behave like a person who has depression, you will feel like one. And the mind promotes a distorted theory: "When the depression is over, I will resume my activities." You couldn't be more wrong. The longer we wait for our mood to change without doing anything, the longer the depression lasts and takes shape in us.

Take a sheet of paper and a sharp pencil and write down what activities you have completed in the last few days, what activities you have avoided, and how they have made you feel. Evaluate how you felt from 0 (very bad) to 10 (excellent). Notice that consequently, the problem is getting worse for two central reasons: *we avoid activities that would give us good results, positive emotions, and significance,* and *we live according to emotional states, not according to our values and goals.*

Why do we do behavioral activation?

Through behavioral activation, we reduce depression and regain the meaning of living.

According to recent studies summarized by Leahy 2017, behavioral activation has remarkable effects in reducing the symptoms of depression.[15]

Behavioral activation refers to the fact that we plan and perform repeated activities, even if we feel bad. There are only two alternatives: **to live life as dictated by depression or to live life in an antidepressant way.** We can admit we feel very sad; we accept that these are the problems, but we do completely differently than depression tells us. Despite the fact that depression tells us nothing is interesting to do, we make plans and apply them.

It is normal for this to be difficult at first, for our actions to overwhelm us, and for our depression to stop us. But gradually, patiently, continuing to perform these actions will become more natural and easier, and depression will diminish. Through repeated and systematic **ACTION,** we change the depressive mood.

Antidepressant actions

Actions that have the power to fight depression have three major characteristics: **they make us feel better; they make**

sense, and ultimately help us achieve good results. The moment we start deliberately planning these actions, the chances of completing them increase significantly.

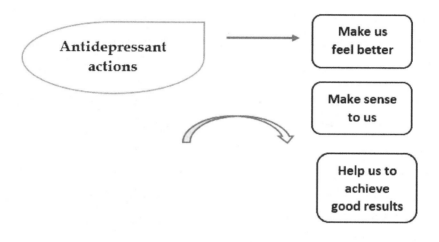

Figure 3.3.

How to proceed?

Choose a certain place and a specific time of the day to plan your actions for the next day. Let's say evening. Make this planning a good, sacred habit. Take a sheet of paper and a pen and write down the activities you want to do the next day. Most likely, depression will tell you to do a few activities at long intervals. You have the right to be rebellious in this matter. Do not listen to that voice. Write down the actions in the simplest and clearest terms possible. This will help you accomplish every one of them more easily.[16]

For instance: *To wake up and read a short passage from the Bible, meet a dear brother, practice the guitar, listen to my favorite songs, plant a tree in the garden, ride a bike, read a great book, pay attention to nature, go out and do good for someone that needs it more than I do, to cook something good, hug my loved ones, to knit, to compose a poem, to look at old photos, to drink coffee and to enjoy its strong smell and fascinating taste, or to go to work.*

You can build your own list. Start with things that are neither too heavy nor too simple, appropriate, and realistic. Once you have a list of what you like, schedule each activity at a specific time. For example, today I woke up at 7 o'clock and read a short chapter from an amazing book until 8 o'clock. From 8 to 9 o'clock, I cook pancakes for the family, and from 9 to 5, I go to work.

Principle to be respected as if your life depends on it

Once you have planned the actions, there is nothing to reflect on or negotiate. First, you execute, then you feel. You don't have to feel like you want to do them. You just need to execute them whether there are feelings of uselessness, fatigue, despair, or helplessness. Most of the time, you will feel that you can't do them and you don't like them. It is normal when we are depressed. *The reasoning is simple: we do, and then gradually, we get to feel.* Studies show us that a repetition of at least three weeks is needed for the symptoms of depression to decrease in intensity and frequency.[17]

When depression creeps into our minds, the arguments become weak, unimportant, and extremely difficult to penetrate. Emotions become so intense that they can bring down any reasoning, no matter how noble it is. Now the main arguments that have an effect are the actions. Allow the pain to leave your mind.

Therefore: STOP with reflection and **START** with action!

2. Changing the way you look at yourself (i.e., attitude towards yourself)

When we are depressed, we have to choose between these two: WE LIVE AGAINST OURSELVES or WE LIVE ON OUR OWN SIDE.

What does it mean to live against ourselves?

- In brief, we fight against ourselves if we choose to see all our defeats instead of looking at the beautiful and successful things in our lives. At the same time, we are against ourselves when we look at all inadequacy instead of looking at our strong points.
- To be against yourself means to use excessively toxic self-criticism.
- To blame yourself for what you have or haven't done.
- To consider that any action you take is useless and meaningless.

What does it mean to be on our own side?

- To believe even if we don't have any proof at the moment.
- To understand that our failures do not define who we are and those failures provide us with great opportunities to learn the things we didn't know.
- To stop being our own worst enemy by eliminating self-destructive thoughts and starting to find solutions.
- Instead of doing nothing and feeling pity for yourself, go out there and try things.

Now, obviously, the easiest thing you can do is to be against you. It's simple to be against yourself. You don't have to do anything or change anything. The best recipe for failure is to just watch and see what happens. By doing so, things will get worse and worse.

With that being said, if you have decided to be on your own side, this good decision must be followed up with certain actions and to walk your talk. Taking action will obviously be more demanding at first, but in the end, the battle is yours.

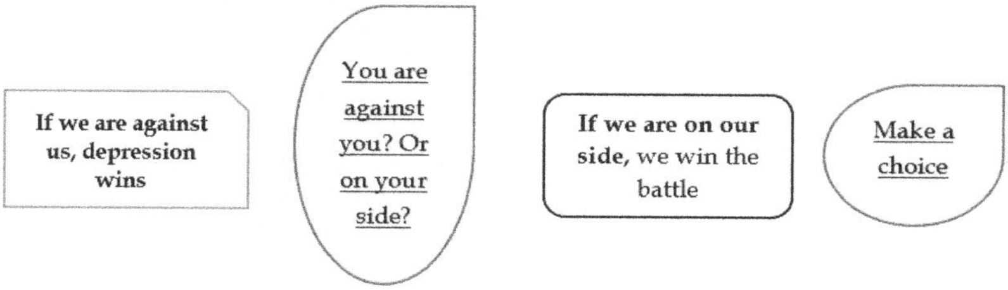

Figure 3.4.

For those who have decided to be on their own side and not against themselves, I have created some **golden rules:**

1. The first golden rule: Always put your money on yourself.

When you choose to bet a good chunk of money on yourself, it means you are serious, and without saying so, you are taking a risk. You can either lose or win. If you are not willing to bet, you cannot lose or win. Therefore, take advantage of all resources you may possess: time, the right mentality, skills you may have, and positive emotions. Use all of these tools you have available, and you will have a greater chance to succeed.

2. The second golden rule: Love yourself and talk to yourself the same way you talk with a loved one.

Think about the way you talk with someone you truly love and have the same kind of conversations with yourself.

What are the specific words you typically use with a person you really care about?

- I trust you, and I believe in you because I love you.
- Of course, you have your flaws, but your qualities way outnumber your flaws.
- Whatever I need to do for you to get better, I will do it without any hesitation.
- Even if you are going through hard times, your value is the same.

Write down what other things you might say to a person you love.

Sometimes the way we speak with ourselves is unpleasant. How do you speak with your own mind? I invite you to watch a video sequence about overcoming your bad inner voices.[18]

When fighting depression, negative voices from our past will start to show up. These voices can take different shapes:

words, images, and scenarios. These voices tend to modify our perception because we have allowed them to control us in the past and accept them as truth. In reality, our negative self-talk is depression lying to us. Through repetition, they've become a mental habit. We can replace these lies by creating another positive automatism. You can start right now. Start by creating a simple and clear sentence, i.e., "I believe in myself, I can do better." Repeat this phrase every day for the next week in the morning and evening before you brush your teeth. You don't necessarily need to believe in it. Remember the saying fake it until you make it? It works.

3. The third golden rule: Be mindful of your qualities

Although we may possess many traits, oftentimes, we tend to focus on our flaws or the skills we wish to have. We also tend to blame ourselves for those fields where we lack knowledge and strive to get better results. Now is a good time to change our strategy. Write down your qualities. If you cannot think of your qualities, ask someone who knows you better. When a new positive trait pops up, add it to your list.

After you have a long list of your positive traits, pick one of those qualities and do something every day that can make it even stronger. For example, I have promised that I will go swimming on Monday, and I will keep my promise. I promised that I would help my best friend on Wednesday and I will for sure do it. Do exactly what you said you were going to do for the rest of the week.

4. The fourth golden rule: Set clear goals.

In other words, do the opposite of what your depression dictates. Depression tends to cancel your objectives; it will tell you that it is not worth it, and your plans don't have any meaning. Those who have a clear vision also have a purpose that is worth fighting for. If you know your goals, break them down and make them simple. If another person reads your goals, they will know exactly what actions are required to accomplish them. If you don't know what your goals are, picture 20 years from now. You look at your life with pride and thankfulness. Write a letter to your younger self in which you will share what you accomplished. You can now be proud and at peace with yourself. Every day, take an action that will take you closer to the picture you have created in your mind. Take all resources you have available and make them work together. Remember that you have bet all of your money on yourself; play your hand.

5. The fifth golden rule: Accept your defeat

Even if we have failed in our attempts, our value doesn't change. Our failures can be painful, but we learn how to become a better version of ourselves through them. Those failures can be a great opportunity to learn different things about our minds. We change whatever we can change and accept what we cannot change. There are a lot of great people who have made something wonderful with losses. Take a look.[19]

Therefore, you can use these two cognitive behavioral techniques to fight and beat your depression. Try to do more of the things that you love, even if you don't feel like it. And finally, choose to follow the golden rules and to be on your own side, not against yourself. Use every resource available to you in the fight against depression. In the next chapter, our focus will be on how to fight and challenge certain unhelpful thoughts.

4

WINNING THE BATTLE AGAINST
BAD THOUGHTS

> "*Watch your thoughts, they become words. Watch your words, they become actions. Watch your actions, they become habits. Watch your habits, they become character. Watch your character, it becomes your destiny.*"

— LAO TZU

In the previous chapters, I pointed out an interesting thing about how our mind works. Between what happens and what we feel, arise thoughts and interpretations of the mind. In other words, the emotions we feel are generated and projected by our thoughts.

What really happens matters

I don't want to say that situations cannot be painful by themselves. Reality matters a lot, but it does not determine our reactions. When we bring thoughts into the question, the problem is they act by highlighting certain aspects of reality and ignoring others. Some thoughts will help us feel good, while others make us feel bad. The truth is that many of the thoughts we have are voices that have been built since childhood. Our beliefs come either from certain experiences or from the attitudes and behaviors of those who surrounded us from an early age.

In this chapter, we will learn how to challenge and change our thinking patterns. Some of our thinking patterns are so habitual that it is automatic, and just like driving, when things are automatic, we might not be conscious of them.

HOW DO WE PROCEED? ICAR PROCEDURE

I'm not going to lie to you. Working with thoughts is difficult and demanding. Most patients run away from this exhausting phase. It is the main reason why depression, anxiety, anger, or other problems won't leave. But if we are not willing to change our thinking pattern—which is what usually causes and maintains this kind of problem—it will always run after us, and we will end up feeling worse and worse.

The **ICAR** procedure has four fundamental stages:

- **IDENTIFICATION (I)**
- **COUNTERING (C)**
- **ALTERNATIVES (A)**
- **REPETITION (R)**

▶ IDENTIFICATION (I)

In the first stage, the goal is to identify thoughts that bother us. We can do this by analyzing our inner language. What things do we communicate with ourselves when we are depressed, anxious, or angry?

Below are some examples of thoughts that may arise during difficult times: "I have disappointed everyone. I am a weight on others' shoulders. I'm guilty of causing everything that happens to me. Nobody really cares about me. I'm a total failure. Nobody needs me."

Beneath is a list of the most common thoughts that pop up when the mind is troubled. I challenge you to look at the list and invest time in identifying specific problems in your thinking life. Complete the list according to other thoughts that bother you.

Possible unhelpful thoughts[1]

- 1. I'm not good at anything.
- 2. Nobody cares about me.

- 3. I disappoint everyone.
- 4. I am a very weak person.
- 5. I am truly a burden to others.
- 6. I can't do anything.
- 7. I don't like myself.
- 8. My life is a great failure.
- 9. Nobody loves me.
- 10. The world is very bad.
- 11. Nothing makes sense anymore.
- 12. I am guilty of causing everything that happens.

▶ COUNTERING (C)

The challenge with counteracting these automatic beliefs involves a change in attitude.[2] The events we went through may be painful and difficult to accept. But we must deal with whatever happened to us. By counteracting bad thoughts, those thoughts will lose their power. For someone tired and hit by the onslaught of thoughts, this countering process is one of the most difficult things to do. **However, we must challenge ourselves to do the hard work to recover.** Below, I will share with you several ways we can confront our thoughts:

1. Counteracting at the behavioral level

This can be done using behavioral experiments or doing the exact opposite of what bad thoughts tell you to do.

Counteracting through behavioral experiments involves creating experiences through which we can test, directly, through facts, the thoughts that concern us. It is one of the most effective methods because by using it, the mind learns much better than from various explanations. This technique involves choosing a thought and creating a situation through which we can directly test that thought, to see how true it is. Suppose one of the thoughts that surround you and that you believe is, "I am a burden to others."

How do we proceed? We can make a list of five people and ask them if we are really a burden to them. You will be surprised when you realize how much your thoughts can differ from reality. Behavioral experiments are based on the thought you have identified. Find creative and suitable variants through which you can test the validity of your thoughts or what your mind invents.

Counteracting by technique: Do the exact opposite of what your mind tells you

This is a useful strategy because it shows us we can initiate an action opposite to the thought we have in mind. For example, if our thoughts tell us to flee into the desert and isolate ourselves from everyone, we do the exact opposite, deliberately seeking contact with others. If the thought tells us that nothing makes sense, we do something meaningful and valuable that makes sense. You can use both behavioral experiment strategies or do the exact opposite of what your mind tells you, depending on the type of thought that upsets you.

2. Counteracting at the mind level

This is one of the most used and current tools for disputing thoughts in psychotherapy. The most common techniques for restructuring our thoughts are *evidence analysis, logical analysis, pragmatic analysis, metaphors, and narratives.*[3]

Evidence analysis

Suppose the thought that stops you from doing something to feel better is, "Nothing makes me feel better." Our task is to see if this thought is supported by evidence. Simply said, let's think about questioning this idea. Was there anything today or yesterday that made me feel better? Most of the time, you will be surprised to find that there were such things, whether it's a tea you drank, a walk, or a person you talked to.

Use the questions to analyze the thought: Is there really nothing I do that makes me feel a little better? In this way, you will notice how the stability of the thought begins significantly to falter.

Remember. You are like a great lawyer, asking all kinds of questions that challenge your thoughts, beliefs and expectations, ultimately testing and challenging whether or not they stand true and whether they help or hinder you.

Logical analysis

This involves making a correction to the general conclusions that we have drawn from a particular event. There is a great possibility we are wrong when we come to conclusions such as "Life is a burden. God forgot about me. Nobody cares about me." When we come to such conclusions, we do so because we extract a general rule applied to a specific situation.

Use questions to examine thoughts and correct erroneous conclusions. For instance:

- Has life always been a burden?
- Is it logical to think that it is a burden just because I am going through a difficult situation right now?
- Is there another alternative to this thought?
- How might someone else view the situation?

Pragmatic analysis

This is one of the strategies that patients prefer the most. This involves examining the usefulness of a thought. Suppose that the evil thought is the following: "I'm usually not good at anything, it makes absolutely no sense to try anything else."

The next step is to look at the impact this thought has on you. Does thinking like this really help you? How do you feel when you assume you are a nobody and nothing that you do is relevant? When this thought comes to mind, which actions follow it?

Metaphors and narratives

When bad thoughts attack our minds, what we can do is use the resources we have. For example, we can read a suitable parable, listen to a testimony, read a story, watch a movie, read a psalm or a verse that addresses the thoughts we have at that moment.

When reading a parable or a story, your mind can grapple with its various contents. Our minds understand and assimilate narratives much better. This is exactly the reason why Jesus largely used parables. The central idea is that by studying certain narratives and metaphors that have power, we can change our perspective about the entire world.

▶ ALTERNATIVES (A)

If we managed to get rid of those difficult thoughts that kept us depressed, in order for this gain to be sustained, it is essential to formulate other thoughts to replace them. New, healthy and undistorted mental content, a functional alternative. For example, if you believed for a long time: "Nothing makes me happy," a healthy alternative to confronting this belief may be: "There is still one thing or a few things I can do that bring me joy." It can be drinking tea, going for a walk with some of my closest friends or something else.

When you notice the negative thought tends to torture your mind again, remember it is false and tell yourself the true and functional version. Repeat this functional variant until you see that the false thought has died out and no longer represents a danger for you.

▶ REPETITIONS (R)

Even if it's not true, most of the patients I worked with believe that if at some point they won the battle with a specific thought, the problem has been solved. But this is a misconception. If you have reinforced a false thought by repeating it 1,000 times, you won't solve the problem by repeating the functional version only 100 times. It takes repetition and patience.

The truth will set you free, but it must be pointed out every time the lie tends to appear. If you tell yourself 1,000 times that you are a loser who didn't achieve anything but to compensate, you will also state 10 times that there are a few things you have done right, what do you think will have more impact upon you? Those 1,000 times of destructive reinforced thoughts or those few positive statements?

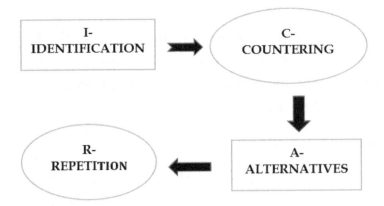

The key is to repeat the entire process until you reach the point where you are fully convinced that you have won the battle with that specific thought. An evil thought may occur in several situations. Repeat the whole process until you see that the truth has set you free.

Dare

I want to share with you this amazing quote:

> *"Bad thinking is any uncontrolled thought. Thoughts must serve us, not tyrannize us."*
>
> — RICHARD WURMBRAND

You may not be able to counteract certain thoughts. And this is normal. But don't give up. Bad thoughts mean bad emotions.

At the end of this chapter, I want to remind you that a healthy thinking life leads to a healthy mind. Negative thoughts cause and maintain depression, anxiety, anger, and other diseases. It is important to remember that our thinking is the most vulnerable area of the mind. I hope you will have the clarity to identify bad thoughts, counteracting them and consistently replacing them with healthy, true, positive ones.

5

COGNITIVE BEHAVIORAL THERAPY FOR SOCIAL ANXIETY

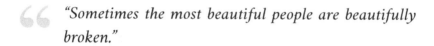 *"Sometimes the most beautiful people are beautifully broken."*

— R.M. DRAKE

Social anxiety is a huge and repetitive fear that occurs when we are present in a certain social situation. The term 'social anxiety' was coined by Pierre Janet in 1903 to describe people who were afraid of being observed while speaking, writing, playing the piano, or eating. People with social anxiety are afraid of being judged by other people or humiliated in front of them.[1]

The intensity of anxiety is most severe when they perform in a social situation. Over time, humans have evolved as social animals. Except for the periods that involve loneliness, we often find ourselves in different social circumstances. In most cases, we act anxiously.

Anxiety makes us worry about future social events.[2] For example, we worry excessively about what might happen if we were to speak in public, and we look for different excuses to avoid the speech. You may feel like you're alone in your fight against anxiety, but the reality is that many people experience this type of emotion more often than you do. If we take a closer look at the statistics, it is estimated that three out of five people experience severe anxiety at some point in their lifetime.[3]

Social anxiety also involves a retrospect of the situation. Basically, we think about how bad it was, what negative evaluations people had of us, and what a bad image they had regarding how we performed.

WHEN DOES ANXIETY BECOME A PROBLEM?

Three major dimensions can show us if we have pathological anxiety or normal anxiety:

1. When social anxiety begins to affect the quality of our life and the way we feel, the boundary of normalcy has been exceeded.
2. When anxiety affects the quality of our relationships with people around us, it is pathological.

3. When anxiety affects our professional results or performance, we are dealing with a social phobia or social anxiety disorder (SAD); for example, when we can't present our school thesis because we are afraid to expose ourselves in public.

The main symptoms of social anxiety are:

- Intense fear of being present in social situations.
- Excessive fear, to the point of panicking, of doing something significant (performing in situations that involve the presence of others).
- Intense concerns about negative assessments others might make about us.
- Constant avoidance is another component of social anxiety. We avoid all situations that we consider dangerous and that have the potential to cause us discomfort.
- Intense physical sensations in social situations (excessive sweating, shaking, neuromuscular tension, tachycardia, speech difficulties).

Figure 5.1.

In the reference section, I have prepared a video to help you get a clearer idea of how social anxiety works.[4]

WHAT ARE THE FACTORS THAT PRODUCE AND MAINTAIN SOCIAL ANXIETY DISORDER?

Figure 5.2.

▶ Vulnerabilities

Each of us has certain predispositions that interact with different dysfunctions and deficits to produce and maintain social anxiety disorder.

These predispositions to anxiety can be of two types: *Genetic* and *Ontogenetic*. *Genetic predispositions* imply shyness, excessive reaction to dangerous situations, the constant fear of strangers or unknown situations, the tendency to be more aware of the negative aspects, and the predisposition to more intensely feel the negative emotions, all since childhood.

Ontogenetic predispositions are transmitted to us by our ancestors and those around us. For instance, by growing up with anxious or depressed parents who didn't support us and were always criticizing us, worrying too much about what others would think.

Basically, if you seek approval from others, you may:

- Find it hard to voice your needs.
- Have difficulty in performing even if you know what needs to be done.
- Think about what others may say or feel about you.
- Always try to please people and avoid conflict to gain acceptance.

The truth is that we cannot change our predispositions. What was done is done. However, we can make great changes at the level of dysfunction by improving our skills along with our positive emotions. Basically, we must try hard to overcome our dysfunctions and deficits. We need to learn useful ways of thinking, behaving, and reacting to situations that help us feel less anxious and fearful. Also, a good therapist can help us learn and practice some basic social skills.

▶ Triggers of social anxiety

A present, anticipated, or retrospective situation can trigger a state of intense and lasting anxiety; for example, public speaking, approaching strangers, talking to people who represent authority, and going to parties or group meetings.

▶ Dysfunctions

These are problems associated with the normal functioning of specific processes which may be neurophysiological, cognitive, or behavioral.

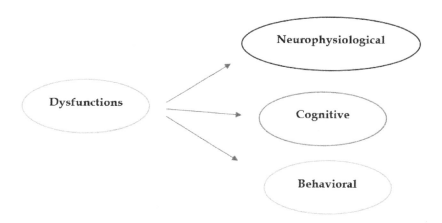

Neurophysiological dysfunctions involve changes that may occur in our body: agitation, blushing, shaking, sweating, palpitations, heavy breathing, wincing, muscle tension, and gastrointestinal problems related to social situations.

Cognitive dysfunctions may result in problems that can affect level of attention, thinking styles, or attitudes.

For example, in terms of attention: excessive focus on your own feelings and behaviors in that situation, excessive concern about how others evaluate you, high interest in what might go wrong in an anticipated situation, focus on what went wrong (feelings, negative evaluations of others), and diminished attention for neutral or positive stimuli.

When it comes to thoughts and dysfunctional attitudes, changes will manifest like this: overly critical and devaluing thoughts about your own person, the belief that the opinions of others are essential, the thought that others are paying a lot of attention to you and what you do, the belief that something unpleasant will happen to you at the next social event, perfectionist attitude, etc.

Behavioral dysfunctions are self-explanatory. The main problems associated with this type of dysfunction are avoiding social situations, avoiding actions in various social contexts (speaking, writing, eating, playing), excessive safety behaviors (drinking alcohol or cigarettes, avoiding eye contact, excessive preparation for a presentation).

▶ Deficits

Deficits refer to the social skills that we lack, which can affect the quality of our life and our relationships with others. In other words, we lack those abilities that can help us cope with social situations. The main deficits that may occur are related to the skills we lack and the fact that we don't know how to feel positive emotions.

No matter how deeply rooted it may be, you can overcome anxiety by practicing procedures that will target the level at which you have developed various problems.

TWO CBT TECHNIQUES TO BEAT YOUR SOCIAL ANXIETY DISORDER

First of all, I want to emphasize one important thing. It is perfectly normal to feel some anxiety or worry in social contexts. Usually, when we see a threat, we either prepare for battle or run away—a fight-or-flight response.

When anxiety becomes pathological and disproportionate, we avoid social contexts, and this affects **our relationships, performance, and feelings**.a

1. Identify and fight irrational beliefs

One of CBT's central goals is to be aware of thought patterns and replace them with more realistic views.

Therefore, whenever you have an episode of anxiety or intense fear, write down in your diary all the moods and thoughts you had. Write down the context in which they appeared, the intensity of those emotions, and what exactly you did (we need to know any actions you take to escape from difficult thoughts and feelings). In the short run, you may experience a temporary sense of relief; in the long run, avoidance actually leads to increased anxiety. Our mind perceives those situations as dangerous.

Use the ICAR procedure from the previous chapter to help you win the battle with bad thoughts. Try to identify the thought that causes you intense fear. For instance, you may think: "I will make a fool of myself, and those around me will laugh." We know from chapter 2 that this is an automatic thought which makes us feel bad. Based on it, we distort reality and try to read the minds of others. Try to spot your negative automatic thoughts.

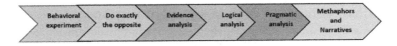

Figure 5.4.

The next step is to fight back against this automatic thought and to use what we already know about this battle. I will give a short example so you can understand much better how you can do this. Let's do some detective work.

First of all: What is the proof that my thought is true? *Is there any evidence that I'm going to make a fool of myself, and those around me will laugh?*

How do I know that my thoughts are accurate? You can do a behavioral experiment to examine this idea. For instance, ask some people how exactly you performed. Can you see any differences between what they said and what you thought? Take a sheet of paper and divide it into two columns. Write down the differences that resulted from analyzing that automatic thought. I'm sure you will have some factual evidence for your evil thought, but there will also be evidence against it.

Other questions to help you win this battle may be: Is it beneficial for me to think like this? What results can I possibly get from thinking in this manner? How do I feel when this kind of thought comes into my mind? When you finish confronting certain thoughts, you should reach an alternative option. For instance: Maybe I will make a fool of myself, but those around me will understand what I meant. Maybe I won't have much to say, but that doesn't mean I'm an idiot. The final step of replacing your unhelpful thoughts with balanced thoughts is crucial. How do you feel now? Therefore, the final step is where you make the change. After some practice, you will probably find that this process becomes easier. So, keep it up. Think of some helpful self-statements and repeat the entire ICAR process. Keep practicing and remember that you can be your own expert at managing your emotions. But, above all, be patient.

Turning your thinking into actions

Not taking action or avoiding certain situations can perpetuate and maintain anxiety because you never give yourself a real chance to show that you can resist/face that situation. Hence, it is very important for you to know if you often avoid certain situations or doing certain things. The idea behind it is to make small changes that can strongly reinforce your balanced thoughts. Now, just keep going. Follow through. Keep reviewing and practicing those helpful thoughts. And most importantly, act on them.

What happens if a certain thought is true?

It is important to fix/challenge fake thoughts. But, if you find that a certain thought is true, you need to examine what skills you lack and start working on improving them. What I want to point out is the fact that we can't fool our minds. Suppose the problem is with deficits. In that case, our mind will know it, and it will be hard to counteract our negative thinking (i.e., if we already tried to speak in public six times and every time things went sour, our mind is aware of the fact that we can't speak properly in front of people. Therefore, we need to start working on our public speaking skills).

Detective work and disputation of evil thoughts are about trying to be objective about our thoughts. It's about assessing, analyzing them, and evaluating to see if they are indeed true instead of accepting these thoughts and believing them without any question. I recommend that you use the strategies that will help you the most. If you are unable to combat negative thoughts, you need the help of an experienced therapist. If you lack abilities, within a short time, there are some techniques you can use to calm your mind and get better results.

Breathing techniques

Breathing is one of the simplest things we do, but it plays an extremely important role in maintaining physical and mental health. The truth is that the quality of our breathing influences every cell in our body.[5]

However, it is interesting that no one teaches us how to breathe explicitly. It is a process that takes place automatically and naturally. Deep and regular breathing is specific to a calm and relaxed body.

The benefits of healthy breathing [6]

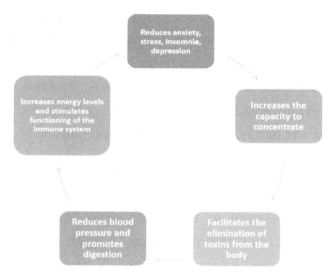

Figure 5.5.

What is hyperventilation?

In prolonged moments of chronic stress and anxiety, we end up breathing faster and more superficially without realizing it. This is called hyperventilation. Hyperventilation is one of the main components that occur in the fight or flight response. It is a very important phenomenon that generally occurs in anxiety, panic attacks, or phobias.[7]

When the body senses a danger, hyperventilation occurs as a defensive reaction to it. This requires much faster breathing than is necessary for the body, which ultimately leads to a lower amount of oxygen in the cells. Therefore, hyperventilation induces the appearance of various uncomfortable physiological sensations.

If the mind identifies those sensations as dangerous, they can cause a great state of fear. Therefore, hyperventilation aggravates the anxiety symptoms because it will produce: dizziness, lightheadedness, confusion, blurred vision, derealization, shortness of breathing, numbness, tingling, cold and wet hands, muscle stiffness, and nausea.[8]

Even if by itself, hyperventilation is not dangerous at all, about 60% of panic attacks are caused by hyperventilation.[9] Therefore, we need to reduce hyperventilation to reduce panic attacks. For the most part, we are unaware when breathing causes hyperventilation. A few symptoms by which we may get a pretty good idea if we are hyperventilating are the following: irregular breathing, repetitive sighing, and often yawning, even though we are rested.

Respiration and hyperventilation

In brief, it is essential for the body to have a balance between the amount of oxygen and carbon dioxide in the blood. Hyperventilation causes a decrease in the amount of carbon dioxide, which in turn decreases the amount of oxygen that can be used by the cells. Therefore, hyperventilation means an imbalance of the oxygen-carbon dioxide ratio caused by the way we breathe.

Breathing techniques for a balanced mind

Studies on the subject of breathing show that less than 10% of people have normal breathing patterns.[10] The good news is that we can restore our breathing to normal. We can learn to breathe normally, be much healthier and enjoy all the benefits of this simple exercise.[11]

The difference between chest breathing and abdominal breathing (stomach breathing)

There is a need to differentiate between chest breathing, which occurs when the main area of action is our chest, and abdominal breathing, which we observe when the abdomen area changes. The basic idea is that most of us tend to breathe mostly by using our chest, which can be a disadvantage. On the other hand, abdominal breathing promotes the widest expansion of the lungs and provides the necessary amount of fresh air absorbed while inhaling.

If you are troubled by social anxiety in your life, chances are you're a chest breather. Chest breathing is irregular and often shallow and rapid. If you're struggling with this kind of problem, you may experience hyperventilation, breath-holding, or fear fainting.

Stomach breathing is usually used by people with little anxiety or those who are coping better with anxiety.

If you breathe through your nose, your stomach probably will expand first, with some little upper chest movement. And this is the best type of breathing, that is most helpful for your body and mind. However, if you breathe in using your mouth, your upper chest probably will rise first. This would show us an unhelpful breathing style and might contribute to the anxiety you may experience.

You have to gain control over your breathing

This calming technique will help you facilitate general relaxation and decrease some of the physical cues you may be sensitive to. On the other hand, you should develop a skill that will enable you to control your breathing pattern.

Note: Abdominal breathing prevents and corrects hyperventilation.

How can we approach things?

You can lie down or sit on a chair with the pelvis slightly extended in front and your arms by your side. Breathe in, trying to use more of the abdomen. First, fill the abdomen, and only then fill the upper part. Exhale and try to empty your abdomen as much as possible.

For this exercise to have the desired effect, it is essential to practice it once or twice a day for about three weeks.

This exercise will help reduce the symptoms of anxiety. However, there is a much more effective technique, namely 4-1-4 abdominal breathing.

Abdominal breathing 4-1-4

Once you're confident about your breathing, you should keep a certain count in your head. Sit in a chair with a straight back, legs slightly apart, and the pelvis slightly pushed forward. Put your palms on your knees and close your eyes. Breathe normally for a few seconds, as you usually do. Then try breathing in 4 times as follows:

- Breathe in through your nose slowly, without haste, counting to 4 in your mind.
- Hold your breath for 1 second.
- Exhale all the air you inhaled, through your mouth and nose, counting to 4.

The exercise will last about three minutes, but don't focus on time. When you finish doing it, keep your eyes closed for one more minute and enjoy the calm and peaceful state that you feel. If thoughts arise in your mind, don't fight with them; let them pass exactly as the clouds pass. Keep in mind that if you want to take full advantage of this technique, you need to practice this exercise twice a day for at least three weeks.

It is good to know that you may feel a little dizzy or may feel short of breath at first. These sensations are normal and occur due to the fact that you are trying to consciously control a process that usually takes place automatically.

Breathing practice

Once you have developed the ability to control your own breathing, practice these exercises whenever you feel anxiety, restlessness, or a state of stress. Before you face situations where you feel anxious, do the exercise, and it will help you disconnect from your own thoughts and calm down more easily because your attention is focused on sensations, not thoughts.

Try to be consistent and practice it every day at the same time, for example, in the morning before you drink your coffee and in the evening before sleeping. The brain will more easily file away this good habit.

The good news is that this new breathing pattern will eventually become a good habit, with some practice. At first, you might find the nose-stomach breathing technique somewhat unnatural. It is important not to be hard on yourself if you fall back into some unhelpful breathing habits. As I mentioned, practice is a key element in developing a more relaxed breathing rate and will be particularly important to help calm your mind in anxious situations.

6

COGNITIVE BEHAVIORAL STRATEGIES FOR GENERALIZED ANXIETY DISORDER

> *"Do not anticipate trouble or worry about what may never happen. Keep in the sunlight."*
>
> — BENJAMIN FRANKLIN

Fear is actually a survival instinct and occurs in response to a really dangerous situation. When a dangerous animal approaches you, it is normal to react with fear. So, feeling afraid is very much a part of the experience of being human. Hence, it is obviously helpful to respond with some fear at specific times, because when we become afraid, our body goes through series of changes that ultimately serve to protect us. This emotion will probably lead us to either run for our lives or become sufficiently activated to defend ourselves.

On the other hand, anxiety can be experienced before an important game, exam, or presentation, and this is a damn good thing. In this situation, some anxiety will boost your attention and will get you ready to compete.

When is anxiety a problem?

Anxiety can be a problem when it is out of proportion to the situation. Basically, it often occurs in situations where there is no actual threat or danger. If we go further, some anxiety might be anticipated in different situations (e.g., an important exam, a job interview, speaking in front of other people). If anxiety is so extreme that it stops you from doing what you need to do, then it becomes a big problem. When anxiety appears at this extreme level, it interferes with how we feel and will impact the quality of our lives.

FEAR VERSUS ANXIETY

When we speak about fear, it is important to make a clear distinction. Fear implies a very intense type of anxiety but tends to be a reaction to an immediate and specific situation. Fear is about right NOW. Fear describes our reactions to a certain object or event.

On the other hand, anxiety is an emotion that can be experienced in different ways, and you may find it helpful sometimes. Some people experience intense fear in response to very specific things, such as heights, water, snakes, insects, or rats.

Generalized anxiety has similar physical and emotional characteristics as fear but may be experienced at a different intensity. The anxiety builds up more gradually, has a high level of tension, and gives you little peace of mind. Generalized anxiety is often long-lasting and may appear when we experience a negative event or anticipate a future event.

This is when a normal level of anxiety starts to become generalized anxiety disorder:

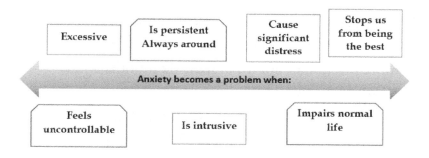

When we experience generalized anxiety, we can face problems like **chronic worries** that won't let go. This scenario occurs over and over again like a broken record. Also, we might fight with procrastination and putting things off because it all feels too overwhelming. In other words, no matter how much you try not to worry, these unwanted thoughts will keep popping back into your mind. Avoiding things is another problem of generalized anxiety disorder. We avoid situations and doing things that might bring us feelings of worry or anxiety. This type of anxiety is not very intense, but will usually bring a lot of tension and long-term worries.[1]

The exact causes of generalized anxiety are unclear but are likely to be a combination of biological vulnerability and environmental influences that contribute to its development.

The DSM (Diagnostic and Statistical Manual of Mental Disorders) 5 outlines specific criteria to help us diagnose a generalized anxiety disorder.[2]

1. The presence of excessive anxiety and worry about a variety of topics, events, or activities. Worry occurs more often than not for at least six months and is clearly excessive.
2. The worry experienced is very difficult to control. The worry in both adults and children may easily shift from one topic to another.
3. The anxiety and worry are accompanied by at least three of the following physical or cognitive symptoms (in children, only one of these symptoms is necessary for a diagnosis of GAD):

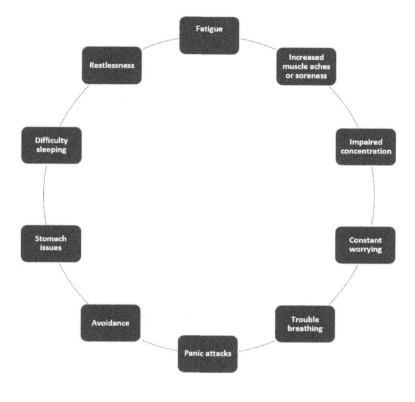

Figure 6.2

TWO CBT TECHNIQUES TO BEAT YOUR SOCIAL ANXIETY DISORDER

From the previous chapter, we know that when a person experiences a negative emotion, like anxiety, it is usually preceded by several unhelpful self-statements and thoughts. Worrying is a process whereby you engage in repetitive and catastrophic thinking about things you predict could happen. Do not forget to **use the ICAR procedure** to alleviate those negative emotions and unpleasant sensations.[3]

Challenge those thoughts that cause you to be worried. Replace evil thoughts with a more balanced way of thinking. Now you have the skill to **Identify, Counteract**, make **Alternatives**, and **Repeat** the whole process.

▶ 1. Physical exercise

One of the best ways to fight your anxiety is through physical exercise. There is plenty of scientific evidence showing that physical exercise can improve our mood and relieve us from the uncomfortable physical symptoms of anxiety. Studies also show that people who exercise are less likely to have an anxiety disorder. Being active will naturally improve some of the brain connections that provide us with the feeling that we are safe.

Why do we need to be physically active?

Being physically active has no side effects; it is free and highly accessible. You don't have to be an athlete in order to be active. You also don't necessarily need to pay a fitness coach. You can train when you want (i.e., in the morning or evening), how you want (i.e., at the gym, outside), and how often you want.

Looking back on all the epochs before us, we can see that people carried out various movements and activities every day. Most of them had a significant impact on human physical and mental development.

If we were to make a brief comparison, we notice that in ancient times human life was very different from what it is today. Humans had to run many kilometers to get food; they had to climb, swim, and jump. They fought various predators or sometimes simply ran out of their way. Nowadays, humans no longer put in that much effort to get food. Nowadays, people drive to work, don't climb anymore and take the elevator where they need to go. They are no longer on the move, being on an office chair most of the day.

The central idea is that although we no longer need to physically put that much effort in to survive, it remains necessary for our minds and bodies to engage in physical activity every day.

Physical activity and health

In a study published in 2006, the Canadian Medical Association Journal summarizes about 50 years of research aimed at investigating the health benefits of physical activity.[4] According to this study, much indisputable evidence of the efficiency of regular physical activity was highlighted. Physical activity has had a significant impact on preventing many chronic diseases: cardiovascular disease, obesity, hypertension, diabetes, depression, anxiety, osteoporosis, and premature death.

The central idea derived from this research is that the more regular physical activity people have, the better their long-term health. Evidence suggests a strong relationship between the level of physical activity and how our health and body will look.

The main benefits of having a physically active life are strengthening the heart muscles, slowing down old age deterioration, reducing heart rate, lowering blood pressure, and reducing the mortality rate by about 50%.[5]

Physical activity and brain health

Exercising plays a huge role in maintaining brain health. Research in the field of neuroscience indicates that regular physical activity helps to increase certain substances involved in the development, repair, and protection of nerve circuits.

One of these substances is BDNF (brain-derived neurotrophic factor), which is positively influenced by physical activity. In brief, depression, anxiety, and chronic stress contribute to the deterioration of neural networks, which is associated with many physical and somatic symptoms.

The substance BDNF allows neurons to restore their neural processes. Moreover, BDNF contributes to the development of new neurons in the hippocampus, a key structure responsible for memory, learning, and emotional regulation.[6] Those people who were physically active reported much fewer symptoms of depression and anxiety, and greater resistance to stress.

Psychotropic drugs prescribed by a psychiatrist for anxiety and depression act mainly on neurotransmitters to relieve the symptoms of depression. The fascinating aspect is that physical activity will do the same thing (release chemicals used by neurons to communicate with each other).

When we are physically active, the blood flow and oxygen in the brain improve, favoring the brain's development. When we are disturbed, physical activity acts as a buffer against damage to the nerve networks, relaxation, and mental recovery.

Also, the occurrence of anxiety and depression disorders among people who are physically active is much lower.[7] In a fascinating study that included 10,000 participants, people who performed daily activities had considerably fewer depressive symptoms.

The benefits were been maintained for the next 25 years.[8] In other words, many controlled clinical studies show that regular exercise has a great effect in reducing the symptoms associated with depression and a medium effect in reducing the symptoms of anxiety.

This means that we have enough evidence about the clinical effectiveness of exercise, and it is comparable to the effectiveness of medication or psychotherapy.[9]

The benefits of exercise are undeniable. Besides the physical benefits from exercise, there are many other mental benefits: mental toughness, improved self-discipline, and giving you that feeling of success. Thus, self-confidence increases the likelihood of continuing.[10]

You don't have to be a top athlete

One interesting study pointed out that combining cognitive behavioral therapy with at least 150 minutes of walking per week resulted in better treatment outcomes compared to a group of people who weren't physically active.[11] So, to improve your mental health and fight anxiety, the World Health Organization recommends that adults exercise between 75 and 150 minutes a week, depending on the intensity of the exercise.[12]

If you don't like going to the gym every day, there are a lot of different things you can do outside the gym. For instance, you can do brisk walking, cycling, running, and yoga; all of these activities have lots of benefits. You can enjoy dancing classes, ball games, hiking, group fitness, team sports, whatever you want. You just have to pick one.

How exactly do we proceed?

Small changes made consistently can reduce the symptoms generated by depression and maximize physical and mental health. Keep in mind that you don't need to exaggerate with it. With time, you will discover those activities that suit you best and make sense to you.

A Chinese proverb says that one who moves a mountain begins by carrying small stones. The physical activities we can perform include general physical activities, recreational physical activities, and high-intensity physical activities.

Choose the ones you like the most.

General physical activities

In this category, we find simple and easy-to-implement activities. For example, walking to the store or a few stops to work, climbing the stairs instead of using the elevator, and doing various garden activities. We recommend doing this type of activity daily for 30 minutes.

Recreational activities

These activities may involve various sports or games such as tennis, basketball, volleyball, football, nature or fitness cycling, aerobics, and stretching exercises. Running and swimming also fall into this category. The recommendation is to do it on average twice or thrice a week, 60 minutes each session.

Intense physical activities

Intense activity is recommended from time to time. This grouping includes mountain climbing or participation in various marathons and competitions. Most of the activities mentioned are quite accessible. You can plan to walk 5,000 steps a day or climb different floors. Therefore, the goal is not for you to be a real athlete or to be a champion in climbing the floors. You don't have to reconfigure yourself all the time. Physical and mental health is based on activities that are simple, useful, and performed in moderation.

Start with small steps

Choose a specific day of the week when you can get a few steps in or an evening when you can walk for 30 minutes. The following week, do the exact same thing, but instead of doing it once a week, do it twice.

It is essential to choose physical activities that make sense to you. If running doesn't fascinate you in any way, don't bother with it. Instead, you can walk the dogs at a brisk pace for 30 minutes. The idea is for you to enjoy these activities, whether aerobics and not swimming, or running and not walking.

A particularly important aspect here is consistency. Instead of striving to swim hard once a week, go for 30-minute daily walks. It takes a lot of perseverance and patience. There is definitely time in the day that you are wasting waiting for TV commercials or watching mundane shows that don't benefit you. Get up off the couch and do some exercise. There is a better chance that you will be able to complete the activities if you plan them together with someone. Usually, the immediate costs are quite high: we get tired quickly and extra expenses can be incurred, but the positive effects are built over time, and the results require patience.

▶ 2. Start to solve problems

To live is to solve problems. When we're talking about anxiety, this process becomes a lot more difficult, and that is because of two reasons:

- Anxiety makes it difficult for us to solve the problems we used to solve with ease before. Instead of solving problems, those issues will rather look like something we need to defend ourselves from.
- Anxiety will add new problems to those we already have so that it can make room for itself in our life.

Problems-solving and anxiety

The way we solve our problems can reduce or worsen anxiety. Working on our problem-solving pattern can surely reduce anxiety.[13]

Let's take a closer view and see how this works.[14]

Figure 6.3.

1. First step—identify and select the problem

First of all, make a list of the problems you are currently facing. Instead of just thinking about them, write them down. A written and well-defined problem is way easier to solve than one that is vague and sitting only in one's mind.

Make an evaluation of three dimensions for every single problem you have written down.

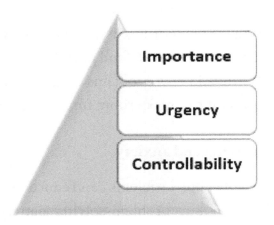

Figure 6.4.

First dimension. IMPORTANCE (How important that specific problem is, from 1-unimportant to 10-extremely important). An important problem is one that brings terrible results if we do not solve it.

Second dimension. URGENCY (How fast that specific problem needs to be taken care of, from 1-not that urgent to 10-extremely fast). A problem is extremely urgent only if it results in high costs when not solved on time.

Third dimension. CONTROLLABILITY (How much solving that problem will depend on yourself, from 1-depends largely on external factors to 10-solving this problem is totally dependent on me and only me). A problem is manageable only if the solution to it depends on your mind and effort, not on others.

Classify the problems based on the numbers you now have. You can use one dimension (i.e., importance) or a combination (e.g., I+U+C).

Prioritize based on how you classified. Start with those really important problems that need attention fast until you get to those that are not important and urgent. Also, focus on those problems that depend a lot on you.

2. Step two—specify problems

Specifying a problem means reformulating it in clear and easy-to-understand terms. For example, a problem such as "I need to be more active" needs to be rewritten such as "I need to go to the gym daily from 7 to 8 AM." A problem like "I need to fix my car" needs to be converted to "I will get to the garage with my car by 3 PM."

Only if we convert our problems to easy-to-understand terms will we know for sure if we have solved a problem or not. If we have reformulated our problems in more specific terms, we now have a direction and will know where to go. It will also become a lot easier to solve those issues.

When facing a bigger problem, we need to split it into smaller problems. We can ask ourselves, "What smaller problems can I solve, so that eventually, I will end up solving that bigger one?" A more complex problem always needs to be approached by splitting it and splitting it, until that problem has specific actions that we can execute. It is way better to take small steps towards solving a problem, instead of just preparing to take some bigger steps. For example, if "being more active" seems like a big problem, let's break it down into small actions we need to take: (1) Get up at 9:00. (2) Get out of my house at 10:00. (3) Run errands between 10:00 an 12:00 (4) Cook between 12:00 and 14:00. (5) Take a walk between 14:00 and 16:00.

3. Step three—generating alternative solutions to a specific problem

You now know the specific results you will get if you solve the problem (Step 2). Ask yourself: "What actions do I need to take in order to get those results?" Pick a problem from your list (Step 1). Write down the results that will solve that problem (Step 2), and now write down the actions that you will take to get those results.

For example, (1) How can I get rid of anxiety? (2) By constantly having a state of calmness and peacefulness. (3) By gaining **control over my breathing**, being active, and exercising along with producing more positive emotions.

When we need solutions to the problems that we have formulated clearly, we search many places: we can look at what others with the same kind of problems are doing, we ask someone who has expertise, or we read something helpful.

Often, we should look at our problem from different perspectives, as though we are wearing many hats. This is called the "thinking hats technique." If we want to understand a house better, we start looking at it from the inside, outside, above, and sideways. The same approach works with our problems; we can understand them better if we approach them from different angles. For example, let's say the problem is the anxiety that we face:

- We know what the inside looks like (the hat that we wear almost all the time).
- If we choose to switch and wear our child's hat, the view will be totally different. "Dad has anxiety. But he is strong because he's my father. He will get over it because he knows how to deal with such problems; he is an adult. I trust him. I'm sure that we will play together again soon, and we will laugh."
- If we were to switch with our therapist: "Living with anxiety is very hard. It's a frequent problem in the world we live in. However, it is a problem we can overcome. I'm here so we can find a way together."
- If we choose to look at our anxiety with our friend, he might think: "I trust in your abilities to beat this kind of problem. You can work hard on yourself."

You can bring other characters (perspectives) into the scene. The important thing is to feel like you understand the problem better, comparing your perspective with other people's perspectives. If you understand it, it will be a lot easier to solve it.

4. Fourth step—execute those actions that will help you solve the problem

Write down the actions that you will take to get your desired results and solve your problem.

Execute. Take action and work on those things you have written down. Don't wait for your condition to change, and take action only after that. It is exactly the opposite; you take action, and then your condition will change. Every action that you accomplish, no matter how small, means a step forward for us and a step back for anxiety.

5. Fifth step—track what you are doing

You will find out that some actions will be very effective, some just partially, and others won't change anything. The most important thing is to learn something from what happens to us: What I did that was good, what went wrong, and how satisfied I feel. It is way better to try but fail than not to try at all. A failure means that we are doing something.

6. Sixth step—repeat all the processes

Monitoring the results will help us identify new problems, define them, generate new solutions, and execute them. The bottom line is that we will proffer solutions to our problems instead of falling into the trap of despair and quitting.

Therefore, we will manage anxiety better if we know how to solve problems more efficiently. Learning different ways to face our problems is the best way to beat anxiety and uncertainty. It is crucial to repeat every step because "A chain is as strong as its weakest link. A chain is no stronger than its links." Even if the other links on the chain are strong, the chain's strength depends on the weakest link.

7

DEVELOP YOUR SELF-ESTEEM

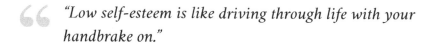
"Low self-esteem is like driving through life with your handbrake on."

— MAXWELL MALTZ

You might have heard and seen some similar words like self-image, self-concept, or self-perception. All these terms have in common the way we view and think about ourselves.[1] At some point in our lives, we are uncertain about ourselves, doubt our abilities, lack self-confidence, or think in negative terms about ourselves.

All these terms highlight how much we value ourselves or our worth. Basically, self-esteem means how **we view, speak and think about** ourselves and the value we place on ourselves as a person. Take a few minutes and write down a short description of yourself. What words did you use? What value did you place on yourself? How did you describe yourself?

WHAT IS LOW SELF-ESTEEM?

When you have low self-esteem, you tend to see **the world, yourself, and your future** more negatively and critically. If you have some challenges, you doubt whether you will be able to overcome them, and you might avoid them. It is possible that you will talk harshly about yourself: "I'm so stupid, everyone is better than me. I'm such a failure." Do you ever think that you are weak, stupid, inferior to other people, useless, worthless, ugly, or you are a loser or a failure?

The point is that everyone uses these words once in a while, especially when we experience a stressful situation or a challenging one. However, **if you often think and speak to yourself in these terms**, then you might have a problem with your self-esteem.[2]

When self-esteem is low

Low self-esteem can have significant impacts on many aspects of a person's life. In other words, a person facing this problem probably says a lot of negative and distorted things about themselves. Also, they might not recognize their positive and strong qualities. They pull themselves down, doubt or blame themselves when things go wrong.

If someone gives them some compliments or praise, they might say something like: It wasn't a big deal. I had some lucky times. If we look closer, often they feel sad, depressed, anxious, guilty, ashamed, frustrated, or angry. If self-esteem is low, you might avoid challenges because of the fear of not doing well. Or you might work extremely hard and push yourself to do more because you believe you need to make up for or cover up a certain lack of skill.[3]

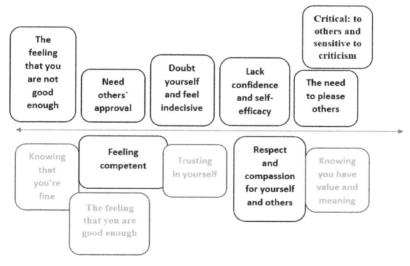

Figure 7.1.

People with low self-esteem usually avoid most leisure or recreational activities, as they may believe that they do not deserve any pleasure or fun. They may also avoid activities where they could be judged or evaluated in some way, such as competitive sports, art classes, or participating in any type of competition.

Having a negative view of oneself

If you're experiencing clinical depression or anxiety, low self-esteem can be a by-product of your depressed or anxious mood.[4] So, you may feel very guilty and worthless most of the time. It is important to have a clear vision of how and why we come to think about ourselves the way we do. When we decide to tackle the low self-esteem problem, it is important to understand how negative beliefs about ourselves are maintained and why these beliefs persist long after experiences that allowed them to develop have passed.

We concluded that we are ugly, unlovable, stupid, incompetent, or made some other destructive judgment through various things that have happened to us (as a child or adolescent) and how we interpret these events. However, now, there are things we do daily that reinforce those negative beliefs that we developed in our early life. For instance, our brain tends to choose what we pay attention to, how we think, and how we make sense of things. But we pay attention to those things we already expect and interpret things in a way that is consistent with our beliefs.

Let's look further, using an example to understand this issue better. For instance, you might believe, "I'm stupid." This belief may be based on your past or present experiences. Maybe you have had some big failures or defeats. Or maybe you've only had big failures. However, your belief about yourself, which started from an initial experience, might still remain ingrained in you a few years later because you only pay attention to your failures when they show up, not to your achievements. Secondly, you interpret any failures as proof that you're stupid. You probably only focus on the times you make terrible mistakes or didn't do something good. You probably ignore any progress or any successes. Therefore, you also tend to interpret the things that happen in your life to confirm your belief (that you're stupid), when there are many other less harsh interpretations you could make.

Low self-esteem and unhelpful rules and assumptions

We learn certain things in different ways. We may learn directly from experiences, observing what other people do or say. This will continue throughout our lives, but our strong beliefs are often developed early in life.[5] If we have a very negative image of ourselves, it is likely that we have encountered a variety of negative experiences that might be responsible for creating this reality. What early experiences did you have that contributed to the way you feel, view, and think about yourself? Jot down a brief description of those experiences.

Today, we have no self-esteem, even if our current circumstances are way different from those we had in the past. That is because we developed negative core beliefs.[6] **Negative core beliefs are the conclusions we draw about ourselves**

as a result of the negative experiences we lived in. For instance, a constantly criticized child may come to believe, "I'm worthless; I'm not good enough." In other words, these beliefs say, **"You are this kind of person."**

Below are some examples of negative core beliefs:

I'm evil | I'm not important | I'm stupid | I'm ugly and unlovable | I'm a failure | I'm unacceptable

Figure 7.2.

Given these beliefs, it is not surprising that we feel very bad about our person and experience strong negative feelings. To ensure our survival and keep on functioning, we begin to develop some guidelines: **rules and assumptions** for how we live our lives. This will help us to somehow protect our self-esteem. We often develop rules like: "I must never show any emotion to others; I must never make a mistake; I must be the best I can be." We might also develop certain assumptions, such as "No matter what I do, it will never be good enough. I will never be able to control things in my life. If I show my emotions, I will be pulled down. I will always screw up, no matter what."

Why is it so important to know our rules and assumptions?

The consequence of having these types of rules and assumptions is that they will guide our behavior. What you do on a daily basis is perfect because of the rules you are living by. In other words, you will try so hard to do everything perfectly and avoid getting too close to people, avoid doing anything too challenging, and the list can go on. For instance, if one of your rules is "I must never make any mistakes," this rule will guide your behavior and make you become very aware of everything you do, checking your activities as often as you can to make sure you don't make any mistakes. This means that you are less likely to be criticized; therefore, your self-esteem is protected.

Therefore, as long as you never make any terrible mistakes, have your friends' and bosses' approval, and get good results at school or work, you can maintain an adequate self-esteem level. The problem is that you are putting yourself under a lot of stress and pain so that you can protect your low self-esteem and not feel bad about yourself.

While things might seem to go well on the surface, the bad image you have about yourself is still there. In fact, negative core beliefs have not been removed. They are right there due to the fact they have been protected by your **behavior, rules, and assumptions**. This is the main reason why these rules, assumptions, and behaviors cannot be considered helpful. Practically, they feed your negative core beliefs.

CBT AND IMPROVING SELF-ESTEEM

▶ **1. One path to overcoming low self-esteem is to promote balanced evaluations of yourself**

This involves noticing and acknowledging the positive aspects of yourself and behaving like a person who has positive qualities. Hence, a good strategy would be to write down some positive qualities and then read them out loud. If you have low self-esteem, in the beginning, it may be a little difficult to bring good things to mind, but the goal of this exercise is to help you pay attention to the positive things you do, your positive outcomes, or positive comments from other people.[7] At first, it will be very hard to find these positive aspects because you are not used to noticing them.

When you notice something, and it's really important, write it down. You can make a list if there are many things. To start acknowledging your positive traits, be aware of the fact that you need to write them down. You can also pay attention to your initial reaction to the suggestion of writing your traits down. What did you feel? Anxiety, sadness, fear, shame, not worth it?

How do we proceed?

Make sure you set aside a special time to commit to the task and carry it out. Let's say that time would be in the evening from 9 to 10. It is important not to do it on the run, or while you are doing other activities, or just fit it in around other things. Give it all your attention and the time it deserves.

Don't forget to write down everything. Try to exhaust all avenues and brainstorm every idea that pops into your head. Be honest about what you write down. It is important that you re-read all the things you write in your journal, reading them over and over with a lot of consideration. Finally, at the end of the week, reflect on what you have written. If you fail, feel comfortable in getting some help. Enlist the help of family or a close friend, someone whom you know would be supportive.

If you get stuck, ask yourself the following questions:

- What challenges have I overcome?
- What positive characteristics do I have?
- What are my best skills or talents?
- What do I like about myself?
- How will someone who cares about me describe me?
- What are my best achievements?

▶ 2. Address your biased expectations

When we face a difficult situation, our negative beliefs about ourselves will activate. Our purpose is to examine biased expectations and find ways of overcoming them. By addressing biased expectations in daily situations, we can prevent negative beliefs about ourselves from being confirmed or re-activated.

Biased expectations are negative thoughts and occur when you face an "at risk situation." When we encounter such situations, it is likely that our unhelpful rules or assumptions will be broken, and our negative beliefs are activated. Basically, when this happens, you will tend to avoid the entire situation and try to escape when things seem too difficult or the anxiety is too overwhelming. Another tendency is to engage in **safety behaviors.** For example, you might over-prepare so that you can better face the exam. Or place certain conditions on entering the situation (e.g., leave earlier, show up late).

Let's say that you have the negative core belief, "I'm so stupid." At this moment, your low self-esteem is protected by rules and assumptions. For instance, "I must never let them see my true face because they will find out that I am stupid, and they will reject me." If you are able to live up to this rule, you might feel pretty good. However, when some friends invite you to be a part of a game night, you might be in a risky situation because you will have to interact or show them your skills and abilities. In other words, your rule is about to be broken. At this stage, you could totally avoid the situation by turning down the invitation. If you decide to accept and go, you might start thinking about those things you could do in order to ensure that your peers don't come to the conclusion that you are dumb. For example, you might start preparing very hard or begin to research the game rules, watch some professional players on TV, or read some good material if things are not turning out well, or you may decide to leave the game.

Challenging bad expectations

In CBT, this is called disputation. Our thoughts and expectations are often opinions we have learned, rather than true facts. Hence, they can be questioned and should not be accepted if they are causing us pain and distress. Disputing your bad thoughts or expectations means that you dissect them and evaluate how accurate they are. Basically, we examine what evidence we have, and we look at any positive things we may be ignoring.

The best way is to write them down. So, to make the process simple, you can use your **thought diary for bad expectations.** First of all, you have to identify your bad expectations and make it easy to ask yourself a few questions. What am I predicting or what am I expecting in this situation? What conclusions am I expecting?

Second, after you have written it down, you need to continue and ask yourself: How strongly do I believe this will occur? You can rate the strength of this thought from 0 to 10.

What emotions do I feel, and how intense are these feelings (sadness, guilt, shame, fear)? You can rate the intensity of your emotions from 0 to 10. Once you have done the first steps, you are ready to challenge your bad expectations. Here are some questions that will make it easier:

- What is the evidence that sustains my thoughts?
- Are there proofs against my thoughts?
- How likely is it that what I'm thinking will actually happen? Rate 0-10.
- What is the best thing that could happen?
- What is the worst thing that could happen?
- What do I most expect will happen?
- If the worst thing happens, what can I do to cope?

I want to highlight an important aspect. The aim of doing this is to make you look at your situation from a fair point of view. Therefore, after you have generated some answers to these questions, you can simply ask yourself: What would be a more realistic approach? Finally, after having the right answers, re-rate how much you now believe in the initial, biased expectations. What is the intensity of the emotions now?

This will help you approach events or situations with an open mind and try some new things, and why not? Sometimes you will be surprised by what you find, instead of letting your negative thoughts about yourself interfere with how you live your life.

▶ 3. Do experiments with bad expectations

At this stage, we need to learn how to challenge bad expectations and test them out to see how accurate they really are.

First of all, you need to be fully aware of your unrealistic expectations. If you have completed a diary of thoughts, you already know what the difficult situations are and what things you believe will happen. It is important to write down exactly how you will figure out if your expectations will come true. How exactly would it happen?

For instance: My friends asked me if I wanted to go out to play soccer. But my bad expectations are as follows: I will lose, and everyone will see how idiotic I am. Then write how strongly you believe in this (from 0 to 10), for example, "8". How would I know if what I was thinking (my bad expectations) is true? Well, I wouldn't win a game, and everybody will win except me. Hence, my friends will make fun of me, and I will feel horrible.

Step 2: Identify your unhelpful behaviors

Next, you have to identify and clarify what unhelpful behavior you might be engaging in to cope with your bad predictions. For instance, escape, avoidance, and safety behaviors: over-preparing for games, reading news, forums, watching TV, establishing some conditions before going: I will play if I am 100% sure about winning and having an escape plan.

Step 3: Remember your realistic thoughts

Repeat to yourself the new perspective that you developed from your disputation, as you will also want to test a new realistic expectation against your old and bad expectations.

For instance: It is just a board game. Anyway, they are my friends, and we meet just to have some fun, and I don't really care about winning. It is likely that I could win a few games too, and how I do at a game isn't a reflection of who I am.

Step 4: Identify your helpful behaviors

This will generally involve confronting rather than avoiding situations, staying rather than running away, and stopping safety behaviors to see how you handle things without imposing restrictions.

If your friends are not doing any preparation for the game, do the same thing and go without preparing beforehand. Try to stay at the game until the end. Play with passion, even if you are not totally certain.

Step 5: Evaluate the results

The final step is to reflect on what actually happened and how this compares to what you expected in the beginning.

To do that, you must answer these questions:

1. What actually happened?
2. To what extent did my bad expectations come true? (0-10)
3. How was it, or how did you feel after acting differently?
4. What did I learn?

It is important to understand that not every thought we have is inaccurate. However, we often have problems related to low self-esteem due to our thinking. In other words, we predict negative things about ourselves all the time. This is a bad habit that needs to be addressed. Behaving in a manner that is inconsistent with your bad thinking is the path to overcoming this negative situation. When you do these three exercises, you will start to gather new information about your own person, which will allow you to see yourself in a less harsh, more accurate manner, and in a kinder light.

8

CBT AND WHAT YOU ARE LIVING FOR

> "In the end, we only regret the chances we didn't take."
>
> — LEWIS CARROLL

Each of us lives in a certain existential noise. We have many tasks that need to be done every day and a lot of automatic stuff. Because we are busy with these many tasks, we often forget *the essentials (what is really important)*. **What do we live for? What are our values? Did we live our lives, or did we live according to a script written by others** such as our employer, neighbors, parents, or girlfriend?

Living to please others leads to anxiety, depression, and all kinds of negative states. It is, therefore, essential to rediscover our values. Knowing our values means that we have a direction and a flag for which we live and for which we fight. By redis-covering our own values, we counteract anxiety and other mental problems.[1]

HOW CAN WE DISCOVER OUR OWN VALUES?

▶ **1. Simply ask yourself what is valuable to you**

This is a question worth answering. What really matters to me? The first thoughts you will have are the ones that have been communicated to you hundreds and hundreds of times. You may consider those things that were passed on to you by authority figures. Have patience. While not forgetting to have patience, try to determine what it is worth living for. It is a difficult and uncomfortable thing to do, but the prize is huge. If it is too hard, you can try to use this instrument (https://www.viacharacter.org/).

▶ **2. Write on some cards the things that are really important**

Take a standard sheet of paper, divide it into four equal parts, and then again into another four. Make eight or ten cards. On each of them, write something that is important to you: health, money, success, career, children, or friendship. **Don't rush—sit, reflect, and think**. After you have written them, place them on a table in front of you. Next, we will use a strategy called "forced choice."

Every one and a half minutes, put one of the cards aside. It's like giving up that value: I can live life without money. I can live without eroticism. After another one and a half minutes, put aside something else. Every one and a half minutes, take out a certain value. Put the card aside, even if you're conflicted.

That way, you'll end up with one on the table. The one you kept last has a rank of one. Give all the other cards a number in the exact order you left them. So, you get to a ranking built by eliminating certain options.

Once you have this ranking, write it down in a column, look at an ordinary day in your life and write down absolutely all the activities performed every hour. You can take several days and make several templates. In one column, you have your values, and in another column, the activities you undertake on an ordinary day. Match. What are the activities you did that day that correspond to your most important values? For family values, what exactly did I do?

Then go progressively. For the second value, what are the activities you performed? By doing this, we're trying to see if there is any congruence between what we think is valuable and what we actually do. It is important to see where all our resources go. If what is presented as important does not benefit our resources, it is not important; for example, our time. If professionalism comes first, what percentage of the day did I spend on professionalism? Is friendship important? Okay, how much of our time have we allocated to friendship? Use examples to highlight what professionalism means. For example: to work 10 hours a day and be as focused as possible.

The inconsistency or incongruity between values and the way we live leads to pathology. **This comparison makes us reflect. What is really important to me? Where do I focus my mind, time, and emotions in my life?** We often postpone reflection on values and on our time. What is really important? If the health of my mind is important, how many resources am I willing to give for it? This process is often painful and unpleasant. But it brings with it the chance to change what needs to be changed. From time to time, it is essential to do this exercise. Thus, we are less likely to live according to a script written by those around us.

▶ 3. If you were to die, what would you like to write on your headstone?

Suppose you die. You need to write a few words about yourself. Here lies who and what? What would be the words you would like to write about yourself? Here lies a person who was a good father? An extraordinary professional? A man who was a fighter? A man who was surfing the internet 10 out of 24 hours? Who was in Zen all his life? What would you like written?

Suppose you are 80 years old. You are a fulfilled woman, satisfied with the life you have lived. Write a letter to your young 37-year-old self. What made you live a happy life? Reflect on what you have done to be fulfilled.

Choose the most appropriate way to become aware of your values. What is the congruence between your values and the way you live your life? You have a duty to discover your own values and live life according to them. Every moment of life is the expression of our values. To live a fuller life, we must be closer to our values. **Step 1: Identify values. Step 2: The congruence between what I value and my behaviors. Step 3: Put in your daily list those specific actions you need to take.**

Simplify values

For each of these values, establish a list of behaviors. What does professionalism stand for? What specific and clear actions do you need to take to be a professional? For instance, I read 25 pages daily from a book that is specific to the job I do; I allocate 24% of my time every day for my professional development.

Once you have established the behaviors for each value, put in your daily list those specific actions that you need to take. **Values are lived and executed.**[2] They are not something to talk about; they are not quoted. They are put into practice. You can self-monitor. Do I have in my agenda behaviors that support my values? Let's see what I did from 11:00 to 12:00 or from 16:00 to 18:00. If you tend to live far from your values, ask someone you respect to observe you and hold you accountable. Seek the company of people who have similar values and actions. By doing this, you will have more courage to make the changes you want to make.

THE MOST RELEVANT QUESTIONS OF LIFE

There are some questions each of us needs to ask ourselves from time to time.

1. What exactly do you live for?

2. What exactly would you be willing to die for?

3. Did I live the way I wanted to?

At some point, things cannot be corrected anymore. It is, therefore, crucial to find the answers to these questions in advance. Use these strategies as a compass to move forward to get exactly where you want to be. Whatever it is, we can't fool our minds. Instead, we can live a meaningful life. We will be happier and have more confidence in ourselves when we live according to what we think is valuable.

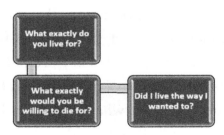

Figure 8.1.

9

CBT FOR MAKING BETTER DECISIONS

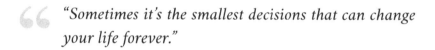

"Sometimes it's the smallest decisions that can change your life forever."

— KERI RUSSELL

When we are assailed by anxiety and depression, the way we make decisions is one of the most important things to monitor. Anxiety and depression have the power to affect the way we make decisions, and so, things start to get worse and worse.[1]

There are three main moments in which the decision-making process can suffer: the pre-decision moment, the decision moment, and the post-decision moment.[2]

1. The pre-decision moment

This refers to the problems and difficulties that may arise before a certain decision is made. The main difficulties may arise for the following reasons:

First of all, a decision can be postponed due to a lack of motivation and purpose. In difficult times, any decision begins to become more heavy and difficult, overwhelming and meaningless. Even the relatively simple decisions: to leave the house, to be active, to read an interesting book, seem to be difficult and meaningless. Therefore, this bad belief appears: "It's no longer worth it, I can't go on anymore. How is this going to change anything?" So, the consequence is the postponement of decisions or what we call procrastination.

Of course, we can justify this postponement for all sorts of reasons. The mind can make all sorts of excuses to postpone a decision that must be made.

A second reason why we postpone making a decision is the fear of failure. We are scared that the decision will be wrong, so we will end up regretting it and feeling guilty. This will lead to agitation that will deepen anxiety and depression.

2. The decision moment

If we manage to pass the first stage and come to the conclusion that a decision must be made, the main danger that may arise is that we often have a choice between various alternatives. This makes the choice difficult. We have no idea what would be better, what our preferences are, and so we end up being stuck. Simple choices that were once made in an automatic way are becoming increasingly difficult. For example, what clothes should I wear today, what kind of bread should I buy today, what should I say when I have to talk? We are in front of a shelf of sweets, and we do not know what to buy. We feel like we're running in slow motion, and we're stuck. We become unable to choose a variant from several possible alternatives.

3. Post-decision moment

In situations where we manage to decide, we often tend to regret the decision made and be afraid that maybe it is the wrong one and thus feel guilty. The main problem is that we are beginning to sabotage our own commitment, and hesitate to practice the decision we have made.

Improving the way we make decisions reduces anxiety and the general improvement of anxiety leads to improving the decision-making process.

HOW CAN WE INTERVENE AT THE PRE-DECISION MOMENT?

Often, our minds can present the following scenarios right before we decide: "I don't feel like doing anything. I realize that doesn't help me, but I still can't change things. Any decision seems too difficult for me." If you encounter such problems, there are several ways to solve the issue.

1. Lighten your decision-making by using your agenda and creating good habits

It is essential to set an agenda for the coming period, for example, tomorrow. Show what you have established to a person you're close to. The main objective is to write down your activities in a very specific way and not to leave an interval of more than two hours between them. Set a specific time to review the agenda for that current day and to set the agenda for the next day. If you have everything planned, avoid debating and reflecting on what you have to do the next day. Doing otherwise will cause anxiety and depression to delay decisions that need to be made; thus, progress will suffer.

Try as much as possible to do the same actions at the same time. By doing so, the actions we repeat will become habits. These habits will become automatic. For example, the mind will know for itself that if it is 7 o'clock, it's time to be active without always making the decision. Even if it does not make sense to perform various actions and decisions, it is beneficial for the mind to carry them out.

2. The stone basket method

If you want to move a mountain, you have to forget about the mountain and plan to start by carrying a basket of stones. In other words, often, the thought that we have to do something big is too difficult, complex, and hard to comprehend and makes us postpone making a decision. The solution is to break a heavy task into a series of smaller tasks and then focus all your attention on repeatedly performing these small tasks; basically, carrying the basket of stones. In this case, the decision is to perform a small task, then gradually another and another, until we reach our goal. If we want to overcome anxiety and depression, it is crucial to accomplish small tasks. Any step forward means a step back from anxiety and depression.

3. Use rules and lists for difficult activities before deciding

For example, before going for a run, prepare your clothes and decide where you are going. When the clock indicates that time, there is nothing to decide, only to practice what you have on the list. In the same way, you can make lists of how you dress on Monday, Tuesday, and Friday. So, when you are in front of the closet, do not make decisions; just apply the established rules: white shirt, black pants. In short, lists and rules established in advance increase the probability and efficiency of a decision. Once you establish a list or a rule, proceed as in the army—it is executed, not discussed.

HOW CAN WE INTERVENE AT THE TIME OF THE DECISION?

Anxiety can greatly affect the way we evaluate different alternatives and the way we express our preferences. In other words, to solve this problem, it is essential to implement the following recommendations:

1. Sherlock Holmes method

Making a decision can be difficult because we have far too many alternatives to choose from. This phenomenon was called by Barry Schwartz, *the paradox of choice*. In short, the multitude of alternatives paralyzes us and stiffens us in making a certain decision.

Therefore, in order to improve this process, we must eliminate what does not suit us and then choose what remains. If, for example, we have too many alternatives for our vacation, too many alternatives for falling in love, the mind sees too many ways to achieve the same goal. Thus, we need to start eliminating from the beginning what we like less. Eliminating is much easier than doing various endless calculations. For example, we can eliminate from the start the people we like the least and then be left with one or at most two to choose from. The basic idea is that we don't have to like a choice completely. This is how Sherlock Holmes did it. He said it very simply. "After we eliminate what is impossible, what remains, as unlikely as it seems, is the truth." We can eliminate at first what does not suit us, and what remains is the best option.

2. Good enough is enough

We tend to always try to make the best decision possible. This is one of the main reasons why we get stuck right before we have to make a decision. If the decision does not involve major risks, such an attitude works to our detriment. A decision that is quite good helps us to move forward much faster, at less cost than an optimal decision. To make such a decision, it is important to:

- Establish some minimum or necessary criteria that a certain choice must satisfy.
- Analyze the alternatives that are available at that moment.
- At the first or second of the alternatives that fall within the pre-established criteria, we stop any type of thinking and choose. The rest of the options deserve to be ignored.

Suppose you intend to get married and have several potential partners in mind. Establish from the beginning, the criteria your future partner must meet. For example, I need to like how she looks, take care of her mind (i.e., read), not be a whiner, be active, etc. Review the potential alternatives you currently have. The moment you notice that two of the people you're thinking of meet your pre-established criteria is the best moment to act. If you were to make a decision at that time, stop analyzing all possible partners. It is very likely that you will lose the good enough alternative due to long searches for a perfect alternative and end up with nothing. Especially in anxiety and depression, trying to always find the optimal decision is not a good idea.

10

CBT FOR INSOMNIA

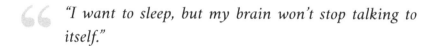 *"I want to sleep, but my brain won't stop talking to itself."*

Often, sleep problems are related to depression, anxiety, or other mental problems. The main difficulties in maintaining the quality of your sleep in such conditions are *hypersomnia* and *insomnia*. Sometimes they are present as symptoms of depression or maybe a precursor to depression. Sleep deprivation or reduced quality of sleep sabotages the body and prevents it from acquiring the necessary resources for optimal functioning.

Sleep disorders can also impact your decision-making process and prevent you from making decisions in your best interests.[1] When the sleep quality suffers, you can face difficulty in being focused, not being watchful, not being able to recall things, increased irritability, somatic pain, poor performance at work, anxiety, or depression.[2] On the other hand, healthy sleep has multiple benefits; a few of them can be: a lower risk of developing depression, contributing to a rapid acceleration in the relief of depressive symptoms, and reducing the risk of recurrence of depressive symptoms after they have diminished.

The importance of increased investigation

If you still find it very difficult to have healthy sleep after you have tried all the specialized recommendations offered in this chapter, you should consult a specialist because certain medical conditions may also contribute to your lack of sleep—for example, sleep apnea, gastroesophageal reflux, and hyperthyroidism (endocrine dysfunction).

CBT AND INSOMNIA

Simply put, insomnia means difficulty falling asleep and maintaining your sleep quality. The main factors that contribute to insomnia are bad habits, overthinking, having thoughts that do not help us, and agitation present at the physiological level.[3]

Sleep problems and inappropriate habits

The first unhealthy habit that affects sleep quality is not having a sleeping schedule. If you want to have good sleep, it is necessary to establish a routine regarding sleeping hours.

We cannot induce sleep through a mental command, but we begin to program the mind to enter a stable sleep-wake cycle by establishing a routine.[4]

How do we proceed?

The first important step is to establish a daily routine of pre-sleep behaviors. Simply put, it is essential to build a habit that the mind will always recognize as the road that leads to sleep. For example, go to the toilet, brush our teeth, put on our sleeping clothes, and sit in bed reflecting on two or three good experiences from that day. Create your own sleep routine.

Another extremely important aspect is to establish a bedtime and wake-up time. No matter how we feel, about 20 minutes before bedtime, start your pre-sleep routine. The mind must understand that the time to rest has come. In the morning, no matter how you rest, get out of bed at the pre-established time. Another important component is not to sleep during the day, no matter how you feel. If you sleep during the day, it is normal not to be able to fall asleep again when you have to.

The second unhealthy habit is a disorganized environment. Therefore, an extremely important step is to build a good sleeping environment. Remove unnecessary noise, excessive heat or cold, uncomfortable bed, or annoying lights as much as you can. For example, you can use earplugs or sleeping glasses, adjust the room temperature, or use a suitable blanket, mattress, or clothing.

Another environmental factor, often overlooked, is stimulating activities that are repeatedly associated with where we sleep. All of these activities can cause insomnia, for example, watching TV while sitting in bed, surfing the Internet or laptop while being in bed, reading fascinating books in bed, worrying, etc. If such activities take place in your bedroom, the brain comes to associate them with stimulation, not sleep. When we sit in bed, the mind automatically needs to know that the only thing that now needs to happen is rest.

How can the mind fall asleep in an environment that repeatedly performs activities that impede sleep? If you are used to sitting in bed and instead of sleeping, debating all possible worries, the mind is unable to fall asleep, because at an unconscious level, there are too many associations with what the mind has to do when it is in bed.

The recommendation is simple. As much as possible, use the bedroom and the bed only for sleep. The mind must associate the bedroom and the bed with rest. In time, simply just entering this environment will be enough for the mind to rest.

The last unhealthy habit is related to inadequate nutrition before bed. Quality nutrition helps to achieve quality sleep. If you have poor nutrition habits, there may be abdominal cramps, bloating, and difficult breathing. Digestive problems can also significantly affect the quality of sleep. It is extremely complicated to sleep well if the food consumed has not been digested adequately. The solution is to avoid very high fats, sweets, juices, coffee, or energy drinks two to three hours before bedtime. Alcohol and tobacco are also elements that need to be avoided, especially before bed.[5]

OUR THOUGHTS AND SLEEP QUALITY

Do you often sit in bed and think about various things from the past, having regrets or remorse? Or trying to fall asleep and criticize yourself for failure or something you couldn't do?

In order to get a pleasant and restful sleep, you need to teach your mind to detach certain problems and worries.

One of our purposes is to help the mind clearly understand that the current day is over, and tomorrow will be a new day. An effective solution is to end the day by making an agenda for the next day. If the mind perceives the day is not over, it will operate in its usual way and will begin to diligently detect various problems and solutions. Once we make the plan and define the problems for the next day, we begin to release the pressure to solve them. It must be clear to the mind that today is over, and tomorrow is another day.

There is a very obvious reason why sleep problems can get significantly worse, namely bad and uncontrolled thoughts. This problem is called *rumination* in the literature. More specifically, rumination occurs when we think about all kinds of things. If we have accustomed our minds to making various catastrophic predictions and reacting with exaggerated attitudes toward our own thoughts and states, it will be very difficult for us to fall asleep and maintain sleep quality. These thoughts will maximize our agitation and prevent us from resting. Moreover, we can get to the point where sleep deprivation feeds our dark thoughts, and these thoughts cause us discomfort and anxiety that sustain insomnia. When thoughts start to affect us, the mind can run various scenarios like the one below:

"If I can't sleep, it must be serious. If I don't sleep well at night, I'm sure I'll have a bad day tomorrow. I definitely have a serious medical problem! Insomnia will ruin my life, and I will not be able to enjoy anything! Everyone can sleep well, except me! Why is this happening to me? There's nothing I can do to sleep better. I am doomed to always be tired!"

One of the patients I worked with, over time, developed sleep problems. Our purpose was to address these problems. The main issue was that he could not sleep and woke up often. From 4 o'clock, he wasn't able to fall asleep again. When I did a careful examination of sleep hygiene, I found that my patient used to watch TV until he fell asleep and did not have a routine or a stable sleeping schedule.

When my client could not sleep, he sat in bed and allowed his mind to be assaulted with all sorts of thoughts and emotions. It took us several months to work on this, but gradually the quality of sleep improved. Progressively, he began to concentrate much better at work, the symptoms of depression diminished, and now my patient can fall asleep much more easily than before. The basic idea is that we need to have order in our sleep schedule, even if this requires a lot of effort.

In conclusion, in order to improve sleep quality, it is important to be aware of certain aspects. First of all, make sure that you have healthy sleeping habits and that you have created a routine that is to your advantage. It is then extremely important to make sure we have a diet that does not work to our detriment.

Finally, the next goal is to learn how to win the fight against foreign and unwanted thoughts. When we manage to develop the ability to control thoughts and relax the mind, we will feel better, and the quality of our sleep will improve significantly.

11

CBT AND HOW TO DEAL WITH EXCESSIVE ANGER

66 *"Speak when you are angry, and you will make the best speech you will ever regret."*

— AMBROSE BIERCE

At one point, each of us has felt angry or frustrated, maybe a little more irritable than usual. Anger is one of the emotions we can face in situations where we feel certain strong stressors. So, anger is a normal emotion. It is important to note that we do not all feel this emotion at the same intensity or frequency, so we can look at it as a two-headed continuum. At one end, we have a state of irritation, as when we are bothered by an annoying noise that repeats itself. We have that intense anger at the other end, like when we notice that things are not going the way we want, and suddenly we start to verbalize.

PATHOLOGICAL ANGER

This refers to an uncontrolled reaction. Anger becomes a real problem when it begins to affect our relationships, whether it is with people at work, friends, family, or romantic partners. In addition, anger is unhealthy when it has negative consequences for oneself. The moment we get really angry and make major mistakes, we can end up feeling guilty, entering a vicious circle in which we either communicate everything that bothers us in an aggressive manner, or we do not communicate at all.

When we feel angry, most of the time, the behaviors and sensations we have are quite similar to those we have when we are scared. For example, if we think that people do not follow the rules imposed by the authorities, as they should do, we may feel angry. If we start to get angry, our heart may beat fast; our breathing may become shallow, and our fists and jaw may clench. We would probably blush and it would be harder and harder for us to think clearly. In common parlance, we say that "we are pissed off." Anger can be expressed by shouting, yelling, or swearing, but in extreme cases, it can escalate into physical aggression towards objects or people (smashing things).

If we are to look at our evolution, such responses have been to our advantage, protecting us from danger. That's how we got to react quickly, and this helped us survive. In a controlled manner, some anger can be helpful, motivating us to make positive changes or take constructive action about something we may feel is important. But in situations when anger is very intense or frequent, it can be harmful in many ways.

You have a problem with anger if you feel angry or tense most of the time, or use alcohol or drugs to manage your anger. Have you noticed that people close to you sometimes feel frightened because of you? Do you break things, damage property, or become violent?

If you answered yes to any of these questions, it might be that anger is a problem for you.

What causes anger?

One of the factors that is associated with anger relates to life events. In some instances, we may be more irritable than in others. For example, when we are tired, and someone tells us something that bothers us, we are much more vulnerable to getting angry than when we are told the same annoying things, but we are rested.

Besides, the emotions we feel could be very different from those of our partners or colleagues in such a situation or in a similar situation.

The main explanation for these differences is the way we perceive things. Therefore, another factor that underlies the initiation of anger is the way or angle from which we look at what is happening to us. If, for example, we think that regardless of the context, others should respect us, we could feel an intense anger reaction. On the other hand, if we consider that this is not always possible, we may feel less angry.

Other beliefs that may cause anger issues are those related to the bad intentions of others, their negative consequences, or beliefs about justice and fairness. Another important factor in maintaining anger is our idea about the consequences of anger itself. Therefore, if we believe that anger brings positive consequences, "this is how things are resolved," we could try as little as possible to manage or reduce it.

HOW CAN WE MANAGE ANGER?

The strategies proposed in the CBT literature are known to be effective in reducing anger and are often tested in clinical practice. However, it is important to note that strategies may work differently for different people in different contexts, as with anxiety. So, I suggest you choose the strategies that you think are best for you and use them when you recognize that anger is about to make its appearance.

1. The first useful strategy is to identify the situations and triggers that cause our anger

Once we know those contexts or situations that infuriate us, we have the opportunity to change our perspective on them. An effective way to change our perspective is to think about how we would react if one of our best friends were in a similar situation. What would I say to help her feel better?

Make a list of the things which usually set you off. For instance, being cut off in traffic, your sister leaving her schoolbag in the living room, or a colleague failing at some tasks.

2. Analyze the evidence

Most of the time, we get angry in situations where we very quickly come to conclusions about other people's behaviors and the reasons behind them. Therefore, we can get a more balanced perception to weigh the evidence that is in support as well as against our beliefs. If we find the opposing evidence outweighs the supporting proof, we should try another, more accurate perspective.

3. Distract your attention

Sometimes it is not possible to change our perspective or to get out of a situation in which we feel very nervous. Given this fact, another strategy we can use is to distract ourselves. This can be done using any activity that helps us change our thoughts; for example, we rearrange our clothes in the closet and repeat certain fragments or quotes/verses that help us recall certain memories. If you are stuck in traffic and tend to get very angry, turn on the radio and try to find a song you like.

4. Time out

If we cannot change our view about a situation because we are so angry we find it difficult, it may be helpful to get out of the situation for a short time. When we are down, it is very difficult for us to have a balanced view of what is really happening. If, for example, we notice that the discussion is heading towards an aggressive tone, we can take a short break, or do something pleasant (a shower or a joke) and then return to the topic of discussion. Give yourself a chance to calm down and think things through before you act.

5. Practice relaxation and breathing techniques

If you want to be calm and peaceful, it is essential to teach your mind to detach itself from painful events and not react to all the triggers. Even if we do not feel like relaxing in those situations, it is important to always remember that our minds and bodies need a break. To relax, you can do activities that bring you pleasure and practice abdominal breathing. By doing so, the mind disconnects from those thoughts that fuel anger and will be able to adopt more flexible perspectives. As our bodies are strongly affected by our emotions, we can also influence our emotional state with our physical state.

6. Solve the problems

In the case of anxiety, I have noticed that it is very important to make a distinction between aspects that are in our control and those that aren't. For those things that are not in our control, we only have the option to accept them. But for those we can control, we need to try to find solutions to them. For example, if you always get angry because you can't find your car keys, come up with solutions, and then put them into practice.

7. Communicate assertively

Usually, when we are angry, we express our frustrations and thoughts in unproductive ways. If, for example, you are bothered by the fact that your colleague does not tell you that he intends to make changes to the work schedule, you could try to avoid talking to him, completely ignoring him, or, on the contrary, you could leave him an aggressive voice message. The central idea is that neither of these ways would help you make yourself heard. Therefore, you need to find ways to say what you think without making the person you want to communicate with shut down or misperceive your message. Assertiveness means clearly expressing your point of view without becoming aggressive. Basically, assertive communication recognizes our rights while still respecting the rights of others. All of these techniques require a lot of practice.

HOW TO PREVENT RELAPSES

 "It is easier to prevent bad habits than to break them."

— BENJAMIN FRANKLIN

Perhaps you once decided to give psychotherapy a try but the problems that hindered you seemed to be invincible. It is likely that your goal was to finally get rid of anxiety, depression, or anger, or forever optimize the process by which you make decisions or how you perceive yourself. After reading this book, you have several advantages because you now understand some fundamental things:

- You have understood that a certain level of anxiety, depression, anger, and worry is normal and even beneficial.
- You can correct the bad thoughts that come to your mind using the ICAR procedure.
- You have acquired various skills through which you can solve problems effectively and make good decisions.
- You live life in a more conscious way and embody your personal values.
- You have understood what is happening to you, and now you know how to proceed.

The good news is that it is in your power to continue to use these tools so you can maintain your well-being and the freedom you have gained. I encourage you to do so.

What to do after psychotherapy?

Obviously, we cannot live our lives by running away from our problems or denying them. But we can live by accepting and solving them. Unpleasant and painful situations are part of our lives. These are life experiences that can make us much stronger. When going through different difficult situations, it is possible to return to states of depression, anxiety, anger, and worry. Bad thoughts may come back at some point. But this does not mean that you will be back to square one.

In this book, you have learned to practice different strategies to effectively fight depression, anxiety, and anger, in order to reduce them to a normal and healthy level. Now it is your duty to do your part and put every strategy into practice. The goal is not to give in to avoidance or give up. The biggest problems of life are solved when we face them, not when we avoid them.

HOW TO PREVENT RELAPSES

There is only one way to prevent pathological levels of anxiety, depression, anger, worry, and so on. What you have learned in this book and in psychotherapy must become a lifestyle over time.

In the previous chapters, we have learned a few new things about ourselves, what mental problems mean, and how they can be addressed. I will review them once again:

- A positive attitude toward ourselves helps us to reduce the problems we encounter.
- Relaxation is a source of energy and helps us disconnect from everyday problems.
- Exercise significantly improves our physical and mental health.
- Thoughts have an essential role in modulating emotions.
- Optimizing decisions and solving problems relieves anxiety and depression.

- Living life according to personal values makes us a lot stronger and more fulfilled.

Knowledge is very important, but it produces the desired effects only if it is put into practice. We need to put everything we know into action and build a new lifestyle to maintain our gains and well-being. Our new lifestyle has the following rules:

- First of all, practice relaxation and breathing exercises when you feel depressed, angry, or scared.
- Second, try to identify and correct the underlying thoughts.
- Another important rule is to exercise and plan ahead for activities that make sense to you.
- Fourth, plan the psychotherapy procedures learned and execute them. Decide, don't procrastinate. We learn more from a decision than from a postponement.
- Break things down into smaller problems and attack them by solving them. If the problem is the fear of speaking in public, take the necessary steps to overcome it and follow them one by one.
- Lastly, live life according to your personal values and projects. Have the courage to put into practice what matters and is relevant to you.

Practicing the exercises and methods you have learned through psychotherapy is the best way to prevent potential problems. There is no other method of prevention than the practice of good things.

If there are relapses

Anxiety, depression, worry, anger, and indecision are part of our lives, and as long as they do not restrict our freedom, it is good to accept them. You may never experience anxiety or pathological depression after psychotherapy, but you may return to your old symptoms after a while. If the symptoms still occur, we can do some basic things:

To begin with, it is important to accept what is happening. This does not mean turning it into a catastrophe or a failure of great proportions. Second, review your lifestyle. By acting differently, we end up feeling different. Reread the exercises offered in this book and if these are not enough, contact a psychotherapist to offer you something more specific to the situation you are going through.

The central idea is that it doesn't matter if you have a relapse. What matters is what you do when this happens. Sometimes our well-being, the solution to a problem, a decision we postpone, a new project, or a new attitude towards life can come from a good book we read or from a movie we watch. Below are some books and movies that can inspire you:

Books: *Life of Pi* (Yann Martel), *Meanings of Life* (Roy. F. Baumeister), *The Catcher in the Rye* (J. D. Salinger), *The Story of San Michele* (Axel Munthe), *One, None. And a Hundred Thousand* (Luigi Pirandello), *Stumbling on Happiness* (Daniel Gilbert), *Man's search for Meaning* (Viktor E. Frankl).

Movies: *The pursuit of happiness, A Beautiful Mind, The Shawshank Redemption, Forrest Gump, Braveheart, Pay It Forward, The Gladiator, The King's Speech, The Invincible, The Secret Life of Walter Mitty.*

The fact that you have reached this point proves that you are much stronger now than you were in the beginning. Relapses can be a problem but not the end. Solve problems by confronting them. If you have falls, look at them as opportunities through which you can reconsider what you have learned and thus get better as a person. And, finally, what you have learned in therapy must become a pleasant way of living.

13

NEVER GIVE UP

"Most of the important things in the world have been accomplished by people who have kept on trying when there seems to be no hope at all."

— DALE CARNEGIE

Throughout our lives, we try to make various changes in our personalities. Sometimes we succeed. But other times, we get stuck, postpone or interrupt this process just before the desired changes occur. That doesn't mean that we have failed or things are not working, but that we still have to work on ourselves. There are still some steps and stairs to be taken. In this chapter, you will learn how to produce the efficient and lasting changes you deserve.

PSYCHOTHERAPY IS A PROCESS OF PSYCHOLOGICAL RECOVERY

You can imagine a medical recovery clinic. Until a certain moment, our bodies and minds function within normal parameters. But at some point, over time, this activity may be damaged. It could be that we went skiing and broke our leg. From that moment, we entered the recovery clinic. There we are observed, evaluated, and we find tools and recovery procedures. There are specialists who monitor our recovery.

However, even though they have a high degree of professionalism, recovering our deteriorated functions depends primarily on us. Therefore, we are the main actors in the recovery process. In other words, it depends on our determination. It is important how many times we repeat a procedure (to flex a leg in a certain way, to take some small steps daily even if it hurts). It is up to us how often we monitor progress and what lessons we learn from what is really happening to us.

The same thing happens in psychotherapy. The psychological functioning we have benefited from may deteriorate at some point, or maybe it is damaged. At that point, we can begin the process of psychological recovery. Basically, psychotherapy is a recovery of psychological functions.

In psychotherapy, you get assessment, recovery procedures, and clinicians to help you. **But the truth is that you are the**

main actor in the process of psychological recovery. The success of recovery depends directly on personal involvement in practicing the prescribed procedures and treatment. A good therapist can prescribe, monitor, and guarantee some quality tools, but no matter how good they are, your therapist cannot execute them for you. So, two things are crucial to starting a successful psychological recovery:

1. To be absolutely convinced, 24 hours a day, that you are the main actor. If you don't get involved and don't play your role well, your recovery will suffer, no matter how good those playing secondary roles may be.

2. Change your attitude toward the problems you face. We often use our difficulties to complain, make excuses, or get secondary benefits such as attention and affection from those around us. At this point, the problems must be seen as tasks that we must solve. In this book, you have some cognitive-behavioral strategies and procedures to help move forward. Use the people and resources around you in this recovery process.

Therefore, if you want to fully recover, it is important that you perform the recovery procedures as specified and have a correct understanding of what the change means to you.

HOW CHANGE REALLY HAPPENS

Usually, change is not a linear process. Sometimes the change is robust from the beginning and continuous, without any fluctuations. Basically, from one week to the next, you feel much better. But this is a happy case and quite rare. It generally occurs with mild problems that are diagnosed and treated early. Sometimes fluctuations, recurrences, and relapses occur. Some of them are difficult or almost impossible to avoid, but there is a little progress each time. We don't fall as low as before.

There are situations where at first, the effort is huge, and the benefit is very small. This occurs when we have an emotional, old, and chronic suffering that we carried for many years without treating. However, we must continue even if the effort is big, and the progress is insignificant at the beginning. At some point, all the little bits of progress we have made will add up and produce the expected result. And that's where we want to go.

It's like learning a foreign language; at first, the effort is big, and the progress is quite little. We tend to give up on the whole idea. But if we continue, all these small cumulative gains will reach the desired level, and we will wake up one day at the point where we can simply speak that language fluently and without any problems.

The conclusion is quite simple: Go on. Use Napoleon's wisdom: **"Victory belongs to the most persevering."**

THE THREE PILLARS OF CHANGE

The recovery process is based on three major components: **execution, repetition, and reflection.**

Execution means that we perform the procedures we have described in this book every day, along with those we have learned from other sources. We will only start to feel different if we start to do things differently. Therefore, make it as easy as possible to do the exercises in the same place and at the same time. Sometimes you'll hear the voices of the past: "It's not worth it, it doesn't make any sense."

Just because you hear those voices doesn't mean you have to listen to them. Do the opposite of what you hear. Give yourself rewards or penalties doing what you are supposed to do or for not doing what you have to do.

Repetition means that recovery procedures are performed daily. In other words, they are a lifestyle of good habits. Therapeutic success does not come from the fact that you understand the logic of certain procedures, nor from the fact that you perform them only once or several times. Therapeutic success comes from the repetition of procedures. This is what happens with any kind of achievement. For good behavior to become a habit, it needs to be repeated 18–360 times.

Reflection allows us to monitor the way we work and to learn great lessons. Based on these, we will become more and more skilled in practicing recovery procedures. Write personal reflections on the experience in your own journal. You can even discuss them with those around you. In conclusion, good results involve three major components: **execution, repetition, and reflection.**

Remember that therapy is a process of psychological recovery. You are the main actor in the recovery process. Problems are tasks to be solved, based on the procedures we have learned. Change or recovery is not always linear. Intentions must be precise, and change means **execution, repetition, and reflection.**

Kintsugi—the art of embracing damage

We know that trauma can be repressed, but it can't be erased. Lasting reconciliation is achieved by emotional self-awareness and by embracing the change agents of trauma. This idea of embracing our wounds, our brokenness, is manifested quite poetically in kintsugi, a Japanese mending practice. Literally, kintsugi is the art of fixing broken pottery with lacquer resin, dusted or mixed with powdered gold. Basically, by repairing broken ceramics, it's possible to give a new lease of life to pottery that becomes even more refined thanks to its scars.

The Japanese art of kintsugi teaches that broken objects are not something to hide but to display with pride. Usually, when a bowl or precious vase falls and breaks into pieces, we throw it away angrily and regretfully. The kintsugi technique consists in gathering fragments and giving them a new, more refined aspect. So, every repaired piece is unique because of the randomness with which ceramics shatter and how the irregular patterns formed are enhanced with the use of metals.[1]

With this kind of art, it is possible to create true and always different works of art, each with its own story and beauty, thanks to the unique crack formed when the object breaks. The philosophy here follows from a broader Japanese aesthetic, wabi-sabi, that finds beauty not in traditional Western ideals of symmetry or geometry but in Buddhist concepts of impermanence and imperfection. The fractures on a ceramic bowl don't represent the end of that object's life but rather an essential moment in its history: the flaws of its shape aren't hidden from inspection but emblazoned with golden significance. Maybe Hemingway had kintsugi in mind when he wrote that famous line from A Farewell to Arms: "The world breaks everyone and afterward many are strong in the broken places." The amazing art of kintsugi, a fading art like so many handcrafts, symbolizes an important truth: **Repair requires transformation.**[2]

It's evidence that we're all fallible, that we heal and grow. Exposing vulnerabilities, by admitting errors, creates intimacy and trust in a relationship and fosters mutual understanding. Actually, mistakes can be the most important and effective experiences of all. Things may fall apart. That's life.

But if you're wise, you can use every scrap, patch yourself up, and keep going.

You may occasionally chip and break and need repairs. And that's just fine. We shouldn't throw away broken objects. You shouldn't throw away emotional problems. We should try to repair things because this is the essence of resilience. Each of us should look for a better way to cope with traumatic events in a positive way.

CONCLUSION

We have reached the end of this journey, and this is a good and very encouraging sign. I want to congratulate all of you who have shown patience and come this far, investing in the most important thing: your mind. The fact that you have been committed is a good sign that you care and are interested in discovering how the mind works in difficult circumstances.

I really hope that this book will contribute to a better understanding of the cognitive-behavioral paradigm. At the same time, in addition to the general information about how things work in CBT, you will find simple and useful strategies that you can apply, depending on the difficulties you face in your day-to-day life.

However, the most important thing is not to lose hope and not to give up on the constant efforts you need to put in so that you can develop a safe and pleasant place in your mind. Arm yourself with patience and perseverance and do your best to implement, every day, the techniques described in this material.

Finally, I hope this book will be useful, and you will enjoy it in the best possible way.

If this material was helpful to you, I would be grateful if you share it with your friends or with someone you know who needs it.

Also, in order for me to improve things in the future, you can share your honest opinion by leaving a sincere review on Amazon.

Simply scan this QR code to do just that!

OTHER BOOKS WRITTEN BY ANDREI NEDELCU

The Codependency Recovery Workbook: A12-Week Master Plan to Stop Being Codependent and Start Loving Yourself

Scan the QR code to check it out

NOTES

1. WHAT IS COGNITIVE BEHAVIORAL THERAPY (CBT)?

1. Ferenczi, S., & Rank, O. (1986). The development of psychoanalysis. Classics in psychoanalysis monograph series.
2. David, D., Cristea, I., & Hofmann, S. G. (2018). Why cognitive behavioral therapy is the current gold standard of psychotherapy. Frontiers in psychiatry, 9, 4.
3. *Psychotherapies*. (n.d.) National Institue of Mental Health. https://www.nimh.nih.gov/health/topics/psychotherapies/index.shtml
4. https://www.nice.org.uk/guidance/GID-CGWAVE0725/documents/short-version-of-draft-guideline
5. Hofmann, S. G., Asnaani, A., Vonk, I. J., Sawyer, A. T., & Fang, A. (2012). The efficacy of cognitive behavioral therapy: A review of meta-analyses. Cognitive therapy and research, 36(5), 427-440.
6. Grant, A., Townend, M., Mulhern, R., & Short, N. (2010). Cognitive behavioural therapy in mental health care. Sage.
7. Gaudiano BA. Cognitive-behavioural therapies: Achievements and challenges. Evid Based Ment Health. 2008;11(1):5-7.
8. Fenn, K., & Byrne, M. (2013). The key principles of cognitive behavioural therapy. InnovAiT, 6(9), 579-585.

2. CBT MADE SIMPLE. WHERE DO PROBLEMS COME FROM?

1. Howes, J. L., & Parrott, C. A. (1991). Conceptualization and flexibility in cognitive therapy. In The Challenge of Cognitive Therapy (pp. 25-42). Springer, Boston, MA.
2. Harrell, T. H., & Ryon, N. B. (1983). Cognitive-behavioral assessment of depression: clinical validation of the automatic thoughts questionnaire. Journal of consulting and clinical psychology, 51(5), 721.

3. Beck, A. T. (1963). Thinking and depression: I. Idiosyncratic content and cognitive distortions. Archives of general psychiatry, 9(4), 324-333.

4. Beck, A. T., Rush, A. J., Shaw, B. F., & Emery, G. (1979). Cognitive therapy of depression. New York: Guilford Press.

3. COGNITIVE BEHAVIORAL STRATEGY TO OVERCOME DEPRESSION

1. I had a black dog, his name was depression

2. Diagnostic and Statistical Manual of Mental Disorders, 5th Edition: DSM 5.

3. 5 Signs Of Depression That Should Never Be Ignored (youtube)

4. Fulghum Bruce, D. (2022, Sept. 27) *Depression complications*. WebMD. https://www.webmd.com/depression/guide/depression-complications#1

5. Drevets, W. C., Price, J. L., & Furey, M. L. (2008). Brain structural and functional abnormalities in modd disorders:implications for neurocircuitry models of depression. Brain structurare and function, 213(1-2), 93-118.

6. Caspi, A., Sugden, K., Moffitt, T. E., Taylor, A., Craig, I. W., Harrington, H., ... & Poulton, R. (2003). Influence of life stress on depression: moderation by a polymorphism in the 5-HTT gene. Science, 301(5631), 386-389.

7. Depresia boala modernității. Dr Samuel Pfeifer.

8. The vast majority of diseases do not have a single cause, they involve an accumulation of reasons. Formulated in simpler terms, a glass of water consists of many drops of water. Therefore, depression involves a combination of factors that interact with each other.

9. Fulghum Bruce, D. (2021, March 8). *Causes of depression*. WebMB. https://www.webmd.com/depression/guide/causes-depression#1

10. Goldman, N., Glei, D. A., Lin, Y. H., & Weinstein, M. (2010). The serotonin transporter polymorphism (5-HTTLPR): allelic variation and links with depressive symptoms. Depression and anxiety, 27(3), 260-269.

11. Beck, A. T. (2008). The evolution of the cognitive model of depression and its neurobiological correlates. American Journal of Psychiatry, 165(8), 969-977.

12. Beck, A. T., & Haigh, E. A. (2014). Advances in cognitive theory and therapy: The generic cognitive model. Annual review of clinical psychology,

10, 1-24.

13. Winston Churchill about his depressions (Black Dogs) (English subtitles-youtube)

14. Ackerman, C.E. (2018, March 24). *Learn helplessness: Seligman's theory of depression.* PositivePsychology.com https://positivepsychology.com/learned-helplessness-seligman-theory-depression-cure/

15. Treatment Plans and Interventions for Depression and Anxiety Disorders, Leahy 2017.

16. Brief Behavioral Activation Treatment for Depression: 10 Year Revision (Lejuez, Hopko, Acierno, Daughters, & Pagoto, 2011)

17. Lejuez, C. W., Hopko, D. R., Acierno, R., Daughters, S. B., & Pagoto, S. L. (2011). Ten year revision of the brief behavioral activation treatment for depression: revised treatment manual. Behavior modification, 35(2), 111-161.

18. https://www.youtube.com/watch?v=gGuZVuUBeiQ&feature=emb_title

19. https://www.youtube.com/watch?v=zLYECIjmnQs&feature=emb_title

4. WINNING THE BATTLE AGAINST BAD THOUGHTS

1. Krull, E. (2018). *Depression and Letting Go of Negative Thoughts.* Psych Central. Retrieved on July 10, 2020, from https://psychcentral.com/lib/depression-and-letting-go-of-negative-thoughts/

2. *Cognitive Restructuring* (n.d.) Therapist Aid. https://www.therapistaid.com/therapy-guide/cognitive-restructuring

3. Young, J. E., Rygh, J. L., Weinberger, A. D., & Beck, A. T. (2014). Cognitive therapy for depression.

5. COGNITIVE BEHAVIORAL THERAPY FOR SOCIAL ANXIETY

1. Kaczkurkin AN, Foa EB. Cognitive-behavioral therapy for anxiety disorders: an update on the empirical evidence. Dialogues Clin Neurosci. 2015;17(3):337-46.

2. Kingsep, P., & Nathan, P. (2003). Shy No Longer. Perth, Western Australia: Centre for Clinical

Interventions.

3. Harvard Medical School, 2007. National Comorbidity Survey (NCS). (2017, August 21). Retrieved from https://www.hcp.med.harvard.edu/ncs/index.php. Data Table 2: 12-month prevalence DSM-IV/WMH-CIDI disorders by sex and cohort.

4. https://www.youtube.com/watch?v=OMGUzXknoVQ&feature=emb_title

5. Pal, G.K. Velkumary, S. and Madanmohan. (2004). Effect of short-term practice of breathing exercises on autonomic functions in normal human volunteers. Indian Journal of Medical Research, 120, 115-121.

6. Jerath, R., Edry J.W, Barnes, V.A., and Jerath, V. (2006). Physiology of long pranayamic breathing: Neural respiratory elements may provide a mechanism that explains how slow deep breathing shifts the autonomic nervous system. Medical Hypothesis, 67, 566-571.

7. Holt, P. E., & Andrews, G. (1989). Hyperventilation and anxiety in panic disorder, social phobia, GAD and normal controls. *Behaviour Research and Therapy*, *27*(4), 453-460.

8. Rapee, R. M., & Heimberg, R. G. (1997). A cognitive-behavioral model of anxiety in social phobia. Behaviour Research and Therapy, 35, 741–756.

9. Garssen, B., Buikhuisen, M., & van Dyck, R. (1996). Hyperventilation and panic attacks. *The American Journal of Psychiatry*.

10. *Breathing pattern*. (n.d.) Science Direct. https://www.sciencedirect.com/topics/medicine-and-dentistry/breathing-pattern

11. Rapee, R. M., & Heimberg, R. G. (1997). A cognitive-behavioral model of anxiety in social phobia. Behaviour Research and Therapy, 35, 741–756.

6. COGNITIVE BEHAVIORAL STRATEGIES FOR GENERALIZED ANXIETY DISORDER

1. Heimberg, R.G., Turk, C.L., & Mennin, D.S. (2004). Generalized Anxiety Disorder: Advances in Research and
Practice. New York: Guilford Press.

2. Heimberg, R. G., Hofmann, S. G., Liebowitz, M. R., Schneier, F. R., Smits, J. A., Stein, M. B., ... & Craske, M. G. (2014). Social anxiety disorder in DSM-5. *Depression and anxiety*, *31*(6), 472-479.

3. Barlow, D.H. (2002). Anxiety and Its Disorders: The Nature and Treatment of Anxiety and Panic (2nd ed.).

London: Guilford Press.

4. Warburton, Nicol & Bredin (2006). Health benefits of physical activity: the evidence. Canadian Med Assoc J, 174, 801-809.

5. Taylor et al. (2004). Exercise-based rehabilitation for patients with coronary heart disease: systematic review and meta-analysis of randomized clinical trials. American J of Med, 116, 682-692.

6. Stephens, T. (1998). Physical activity and mental health in the United States and Canada: evidence from four popular surveys. Prev Med, 17, 35-37.

7. Steptoe, A. et al. (1996). Sports participation and emotional wellbeing in adolescents. Lancet, 347, 1789-1792.

8. Paffenbarger Jr, R. S., Kampert, J. B., Lee, I. M., Hyde, R. T., Leung, R. W., & Wing, A. L. (1994). Changes in physical activity and other lifeway patterns influencing longevity. *Medicine and science in sports and exercise, 26*(7), 857-865.

9. Broocks, A. et al. (1998). Comparison of aerobic exercise, clomioramine and placebo in the treatment of anic disorder. Am J Psychiatry, 155, 603-609.

10. TEDWomen. (2017). The brain-changing benefits of exercise | Wendy Suzuki [Video]. https://www.ted.com/talks/wendy_suzuki_the_brain_changing_benefits_of_exercise/up-next?language=en

11. Hovland, A., Nordhus, I. H., Sjøbø, T., Gjestad, B. A., Birknes, B., Martinsen, E. W., ... & Pallesen, S. (2013). Comparing physical exercise in groups to group cognitive behaviour therapy for the treatment of panic disorder in a randomized controlled trial. Behavioural and cognitive psychotherapy, 41(4), 408-432.

12. *Physical activity.* (2022). World Health Organization. https://www.who.int/news-room/fact-sheets/detail/physical-activity

13. Ladouceur, R., Blais, F., Freeston, M. H., & Dugas, M. J. (1998). Problem solving and problem orientation in generalized anxiety disorder. Journal of anxiety disorders, 12(2), 139-152.

14. Mendonca, J. D., & Siess, T. F. (1976). Counseling for indecisiveness: Problem-solving and anxiety-management training. *Journal of counseling psychology, 23*(4), 339.

7. DEVELOP YOUR SELF-ESTEEM

1. Fennell, M. (1998). Low Self-Esteem. In N. Tarrier, A. Wells and G. Haddock (Eds), Treating Complex Cases: The Cognitive Behavioural Therapy Approach. London: John Wiley & Sons.
2. Fennell, M. (1998). Low Self-Esteem. In N. Tarrier, A. Wells and G. Haddock (Eds), Treating Complex Cases:
   The Cognitive Behavioural Therapy Approach. London: John Wiley & Sons.
3. Lane, J., Lane, A. M., & Kyprianou, A. (2004). Self-efficacy, self-esteem and their impact on academic performance. Social Behavior and Personality: an international journal, 32(3), 247-256.
4. Sowislo, J. F., & Orth, U. (2013). Does low self-esteem predict depression and anxiety? A meta-analysis of longitudinal studies. Psychological bulletin, 139(1), 213.
5. Miller, S. A. (1988). Parents' beliefs about children's cognitive development. Child development, 259-285.
6. Burns, D. (1993). Ten Days to Self-Esteem. New York: Quill William Morrow.
7. Fennell, M. (1998). Low Self-Esteem. In N. Tarrier, A. Wells and G. Haddock (Eds), Treating Complex Cases:
   The Cognitive Behavioural Therapy Approach. London: John Wiley & Sons.

8. CBT AND WHAT YOU ARE LIVING FOR

1. Coyte, M. E., Gilbert, P., & Nicholls, V. (2007). Spirituality, values and mental health: Jewels for the journey. Jessica Kingsley Publishers.
2. Peterson, C., Park, N., & Seligman, M. E. P. (2005). Orientations to happiness and life satisfaction: The full life versus the empty life. Journal of Happiness Studies, 6, 25–41

9. CBT FOR MAKING BETTER DECISIONS

1. Kirkwood, C. W. (1997). Strategic decision making. Duxbury Press, 149.
2. Orasanu, J., Calderwood, R., & Zsambok, C. E. (1993). Decision making in action: Models and methods (pp. 138-47). G. A. Klein (Ed.). Norwood, NJ: Ablex.

10. CBT FOR INSOMNIA

1. Harrison, Y., & Horne, J. A. (2000). The impact of sleep deprivation on decision making: a review. Journal of experimental psychology: Applied, 6(3), 236.
2. Peri, C. (2014). *10 things to hate about sleep loss.* WebMD. https://www.webmd.com/sleep-disorders/features/10-results-sleep-loss
3. Geoffroy, P. A., Hoertel, N., Etain, B., Bellivier, F., Delorme, R., Limosin, F., & Peyre, H. (2018). Insomnia and hypersomnia in major depressive episode: prevalence, sociodemographic characteristics and psychiatric comorbidity in a population-based study. Journal of Affective Disorders, 226, 132-141.
4. Treatment Plans and Interventions for Depression and Anxiety Disorders, Leahy 2017, Insomnia pg. 50.
5. Stein, M. D., & Friedmann, P. D. (2006). Disturbed sleep and its relationship to alcohol use. Substance abuse, 26(1), 1-13.

13. NEVER GIVE UP

1. *Wabi-sabi: The magnificence of imperfection*: Cheryl Hunter at TEDxSantaMonica: https://www.youtube.com/watch?v=V1gxziZwmkc
2. Kaufman, S. B., (2014) Scientific American; Beautiful Minds. Are you mentally tough. http://blogs.scientificamerican.com/beautiful-minds/are-you-mentally-tough/